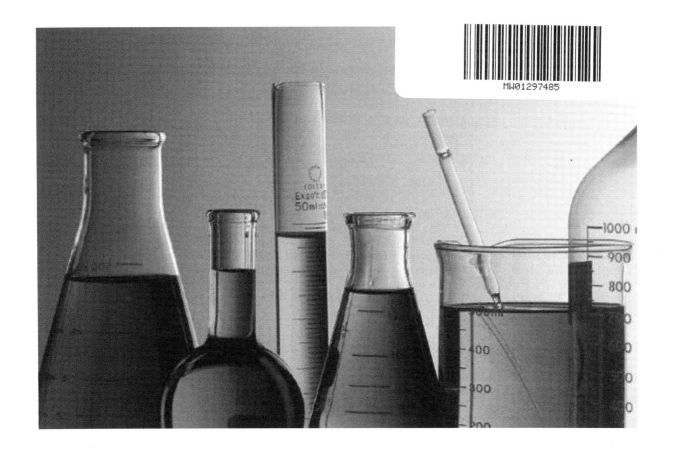

Friendly Chemistry

A Guide to Learning Basic Chemistry
4th Edition

By Joey and Lisa Hajda

Annotated Solutions Manual

Published by Hideaway Ventures, 79372 Road 443, Broken Bow, NE 68822

For additional information regarding this publication please contact Joey or Lisa Hajda at the above address or call 308-870-4686, email friendlychemistryinfo@gmail.com or visit our website: www.friendlychemistry.com

Copyright 1996, 1998, 2008, 2010, 2012, 2016 Hideaway Ventures, Joey or Lisa Hajda

All rights reserved. No portion of this book may be reproduced in any form, or by any electronic, mechanical or other means, without the prior written permission of the publisher.

Periodic Table Of the Elements

Legend:
- Atomic Number → 1
- Element Symbol → H
- Element Name → Hydrogen
- Atomic Mass → 1.0080

1 H Hydrogen 1.0080																	2 He Helium 4.0026
3 Li Lithium 6.94	4 Be Beryllium 9.012											5 B Boron 10.811	6 C Carbon 12.0115	7 N Nitrogen 14.0067	8 O Oxygen 15.994	9 F Fluorine 18.994	10 Ne Neon 20.18
11 Na Sodium 22.9898	12 Mg Magnesium 24.31											13 Al Aluminum 26.9815	14 Si Silicon 28.086	15 P Phosphorus 30.974	16 S Sulfur 32.06	17 Cl Chlorine 35.453	18 Ar Argon 39.948
19 K Potassium 39.102	20 Ca Calcium 40.08	21 Sc Scandium 44.96	22 Ti Titanium 47.9	23 V Vanadium 50.94	24 Cr Chromium 51.996	25 Mn Manganese 54.938	26 Fe Iron 55.847	27 Co Cobalt 58.933	28 Ni Nickel 58.71	29 Cu Copper 63.546	30 Zn Zinc 65.37	31 Ga Gallium 69.72	32 Ge Germanium 72.59	33 As Arsenic 74.9216	34 Se Selenium 78.96	35 Br Bromine 79.909	36 Kr Krypton 83.80
37 Rb Rubidium 85.47	38 Sr Strontium 87.62	39 Y Yttrium 88.91	40 Zr Zirconium 91.22	41 Nb Niobium 92.91	42 Mo Molybdenum 95.94	43 Tc Technetium (99)	44 Ru Ruthenium 101.07	45 Rh Rhodium 102.91	46 Pd Palladium 106.4	47 Ag Silver 107.868	48 Cd Cadmium 112.40	49 In Indium 114.82	50 Sn Tin 118.69	51 Sb Antimony 121.75	52 Te Tellurium 127.60	53 I Iodine 126.904	54 Xe Xenon 131.30
55 Cs Cesium 132.91	56 Ba Barium 137.34	71 Lu Lutetium 174.97	72 Hf Hafnium 178.49	73 Ta Tantalum 180.95	74 W Tungsten 183.85	75 Re Rhenium 186.2	76 Os Osmium 190.2	77 Ir Iridium 192.22	78 Pt Platinum 195.09	79 Au Gold 196.97	80 Hg Mercury 200.59	81 Tl Thallium 204.37	82 Pb Lead 207.2	83 Bi Bismuth 208.98	84 Po Polonium (210)	85 At Astatine (210)	86 Rn Radon (222)
87 Fr Francium (223)	88 Ra Radium (226)	103 Lr Lawrencium (256)	104 Unq	105 Unp	106 Unh	107 Uns	108 Uno	109 Une									

57 La Lanthanum 138.91	58 Ce Cerium 140.12	59 Pr Praseodymium 140.91	60 Nd Neodymium 144.24	61 Pm Promethium (147)	62 Sm Samarium 150.4	63 Eu Europium 151.96	64 Gd Gadolinium 157.25	65 Tb Terbium 158.9	66 Dy Dysprosium 162.50	67 Ho Holmium 164.93	68 Er Erbium 167.26	69 Tm Thulium 168.93	70 Yb Ytterbium 173.04
89 Ac Actinium (227)	90 Th Thorium 232.0	91 Pa Protactinium 231.0	92 U Uranium 238.03	93 Np Neptunium 237.0	94 Pu Plutonium (244)	95 Am Americium (243)	96 Cm Curium (247)	97 Bk Berkelium (247)	98 Cf Californium (251)	99 Es Einsteinium (254)	100 Fm Fermium (257)	101 Md Mendelevium (258)	102 No Nobelium (255)

Friendly Chemistry
Solutions for Practice Pages and Tests
(Note: Annotated section begins with Lesson 16)

Lesson 1

Element Symbol Practice 1

1. Li
2. Mg
3. C
4. H
5. O
6. He
7. B
8. F
9. Ca
10. N
11. Sr
12. Na
13. Ne
14. Cu
15. Be
16. Ar
17. S
18. Cr
19. O
20. K
21. Mn
22. Mg
23. Cl
24. Si
25. P
26. Fe
27. Co
28. Cu
29. Ni
30. As
31. Ar
32. Al
33. Ga
34. Ge
35. Rb
36. Ag
37. Be
38. Se
39. Br
40. I

Element Symbol Practice 2

1. Carbon
2. Aluminum
3. Helium
4. Hydrogen
5. Beryllium
6. Iron
7. Fluorine
8. Chlorine
9. Calcium
10. Nickel
11. Bromine
12. Silicon
13. Neon
14. Chromium
15. Vanadium
16. Boron
17. Sodium
18. Copper
19. Sulfur
20. Iodine
21. Magnesium
22. Nitrogen
23. Potassium
24. Silicon
25. Zinc
26. Zirconium
27. Aluminum
28. Chromium
29. Arsenic
30. Argon
31. Boron
32. Gallium
33. Germanium
34. Rubidium
35. Oxygen
36. Silver
37. Selenium
38. Tin
39. Bromine
40. Hydrogen
41. Potassium
42. Helium

43. Nitrogen
44. Fluorine
45. Sodium
46. Neon
47. Nickel
48. Nitrogen
49. Carbon
50. Calcium
51. Chlorine
52. Cobalt
53. Copper
54. Chromium
55. Argon
56. Arsenic
57. Magnesium
58. Manganese
59. Sulfur
60. Gold

Element Symbol Practice 3

The following numbers should be circled:
1, 4, 5, 6, 10, 11, 13, 14, 17, 21, 24, 27, 28, 29, 30, 31, 34, 36, 37, 38, 40.

Lesson 1 Test

1. C
2. Be
3. Ne
4. Na
5. He
6. B
7. Al
8. F
9. Ca
10. P
11. Cr
12. Fe
13. Co
14. I
15. Mg
16. As
17. 4th column
18. 2nd column
19. 1st column
20. 2nd column
21. 2nd column
22. 2nd column
23. 3rd column
24. 3rd column
25. 2nd column
26. 2nd column
27. 1st column
28. 2nd column
29. 2nd column
30. 4th column

Lesson 2

Element Symbol Practice

1. Li
2. Mn
3. Ca
4. H
5. Ar
6. As
7. B
8. F
9. Co
10. N
11. Ni
12. Na
13. Ne
14. Br
15. Be
16. As
17. S
18. Cr
19. Zn
20. K
21. Mo
22. Cu
23. Cl
24. Si
25. P
26. Fe
27. Co
28. He
29. Ni

30. As
31. Ar
32. Al
33. Ga
34. Ge
35. Rb
36. Ag
37. Be
38. Se
39. Br
40. Sn

Subatomic Particle Numbers Practice

1. C Carbon 6, 6, 6
2. S Sulfur, 16, 16, 16
3. O Oxygen 8, 8, 8
4. Mg Magnesium, 12, 12, 12
5. Li Lithium, 3, 3, 3
6. Mn Manganese, 25, 25, 25
7. Ne Neon, 10, 10, 10
8. Na Sodium, 11, 11, 11
9. Al Aluminum, 13, 13, 13
10. P Phosphorus, 15, 15, 15
11. Cl Chlorine, 17, 17, 17
12. Ar Argon, 18, 18, 18
13. K Potassium, 19, 19, 19
14. Zn Zinc, 30, 30, 30
15. He Helium, 2, 2, 2
16. Br Bromine, 35, 35, 35
17. I Iodine, 53, 53, 53
18. Sc Scandium, 21, 21, 21
19. H Hydrogen, 1, 1, 1
20. B Boron, 5, 5, 5

Lesson 2 Test

1. A
2. C
3. B
4. D
5. D
6. B
7. A
8. D
9. C
10. D

Lesson 3

Quantum Mechanics Review

Blanks filled in order: four, principle quantum number, electrons, layers, seven, first, orbital quantum number, shaped, four, spherical, pear, dumbbell, "fish", s, p, d, f, magnetic quantum number, pear, three, x, y, z, spin quantum number, electrons, pairs, spin clockwise, spin counterclockwise, explain, reactive, stable/non-reactive, determine relative reactivity of the elements.

Lesson 3 Test

1. B
2. C
3. C
4. D
5. A
6. D
7. A
8. D
9. C
10. B

Lesson 5

1. Al: 1s ↕ 2s ↕ 2p ↕↕↕ (x y z) 3s ↕ 3p ↑ (x y z)

2. K: 1s ↕ 2s ↕ 2p ↕ ↕ ↕ (x y z) 3s ↕ 3p ↕↕↕ (x y z) 4s ↑

3. Sc: 1s ↕ 2s ↕ 2p ↕ ↕ ↕ (x y z) 3s ↕ 3p ↕↕↕ (x y z) 4s ↕ 3d ↑

4. P: 1s ↕ 2s ↕ 2p ↕ ↕ ↕ (x y z) 3s ↕ 3p ↑ ↑ ↑ (x y z)

5. Ca: 1s ↕ 2s ↕ 2p ↕ ↕ ↕ (x y z) 3s ↕ 3p ↕↕↕ (x y z) 4s ↕

6. Li: 1s ↕ 2s ↑

7. ↑↓ ↑↓ ↑↓ ↑↓ ↑↓
Ne: 1s 2s   x y z
              2p

8. ↑
H: 1s

9. ↑↓ ↑↓ ↑↓ ↑↓ ↑↓ ↑
Na: 1s 2s   x y z 3s

10. ↑↓ ↑↓ ↑↓ ↑↓ ↑↓ ↑↓ ↑↓↑↓↑
Cl: 1s 2s   2p   3s   3p

11. ↑↓ ↑↓ ↑
B: 1s 2s x
          2p

12. ↑↓ ↑↓
Be: 1s 2s

13. ↑↓ ↑↓ ↑↓ ↑↓ ↑↓ ↑↓ ↑↓ ↑ ↑
S: 1s 2s   2p   3s   3p

14. ↑↓ ↑↓ ↑↓ ↑↓ ↑↓ ↑↓ ↑↓ ↑↓ ↑↓
Ar: 1s 2s   2p   3s   3p

Orbital Notation Practice 2

1. ↑↓ ↑↓ ↑ ↑
C: 1s 2s x y z
          2p

2. ↑↓ ↑↓ ↑↓ ↑↓ ↑↓ ↑↓ ↑ ↑
S: 1s 2s   2p   3s   3p

3. ↑↓ ↑↓ ↑↓ ↑↓ ↑↓
Ne: 1s 2s   2p

4. ↑↓ ↑
Li: 1s 2s

5. ↑↓ ↑↓ ↑↓ ↑ ↑
O: 1s 2s   x y z
           2p

6. ↑↓ ↑↓ ↑↓ ↑↓ ↑↓ ↑↓
Mg: 1s 2s   2p   3s

7. ↑
H: 1s

8. ↑↓ ↑↓ ↑
B: 1s 2s x
          2p

9. ↑↓ ↑↓ ↑↓ ↑ ↑
O: 1s 2s x y z
          2p

10. ↑↓ ↑↓ ↑↓ ↑↓ ↑↓ ↑↓ ↑↓ ↑↓ ↑
K: 1s 2s   2p   3s   3p   4s

11. ↑↓ ↑↓ ↑↓ ↑↓ ↑↓ ↑↓ ↑ ↑↑
P: 1s 2s   2p   3s   3p

12. ↑↓ ↑↓ ↑↓ ↑↓ ↑↓ ↑↓ ↑↓ ↑↓ ↑↓
Ar: 1s 2s   2p   3s   3p

13. ↑↓ ↑↓ ↑↓ ↑↓ ↑↓ ↑↓ ↑↓ ↑↓↑↓ ↑↓
Ca: 1s 2s   2p   3s   3p   4s

14. ↑↓
He: 1s

Lesson 5 Test

1. ↑↓ ↑
Li: 1s 2s

2. ↑↓ ↑↓ ↑↓ ↑ ↑
O: 1s 2s x y z
          2p

3. ↑↓ ↑↓ ↑↓ ↑↓ ↑↓
Ne: 1s 2s x y z
           2p

4. ↑↓ ↑↓ ↑↓ ↑↓ ↑↓ ↑↓ ↑↓ ↑↓ ↑↓
Ar: 1s 2s   2p   3s   3p

5. ↑↓ ↑↓ ↑↓ ↑↓ ↑↓ ↑↓ ↑↓ ↑↓ ↑
K: 1s 2s   2p   3s   3p   4s

6. ↑↓ ↑↓ ↑↓ ↑↓ ↑↓ ↑↓ ↑↓ ↑↓ ↑↓ ↑↓ ↑
Sc: 1s 2s   2p   3s   3p   4s 3d

7. ↑↓ ↑↓
Be: 1s 2s

8. ↑↓ ↑↓ ↑↓ ↑↓ ↑↓ ↑↓
Na: 1s 2s   x y z 3s
            2p

9. ↑↓ ↑↓ ↑↓ ↑↓ ↑↓ ↑↓ ↑↓ ↑↓↑↓↑↓
Ca: 1s 2s   x y z   3s   x y z   4s
            2p   3p

10. ↑↓ ↑↓ ↑↓ ↑↓ ↑↓ ↑↓ ↑ ↑↑
P: 1s 2s   x y z   3s   x y z
           2p   3p

Lesson 6
ECN Practice 1
1. C: $1s^2\ 2s^2\ 2p^2$
2. Be: $1s^2\ 2s^2$
3. O: $1s^2\ 2s^2\ 2p^4$
4. Ne: $1s^2\ 2s^2\ 2p^6$
5. N: $1s^2\ 2s^2\ 2p^3$
6. B: $1s^2\ 2s^2\ 2p^1$
7. Na: $1s^2\ 2s^2\ 2p^6\ 3s^1$
8. Al: $1s^2\ 2s^2\ 2p^6\ 3s^2\ 3p^1$
9. S: $1s^2\ 2s^2\ 2p^6\ 3s^2\ 3p^4$
10. K: $1s^2\ 2s^2\ 2p^6\ 3s^2\ 3p^6\ 4s^1$
11. Ca: $1s^2\ 2s^2\ 2p^6\ 3s^2\ 3p^6\ 4s^2$
12. Cr: $1s^2\ 2s^2\ 2p^6\ 3s^2\ 3p^6\ 4s^2\ 3d^4$
13. Fe: $1s^2\ 2s^2\ 2p^6\ 3s^2\ 3p^6\ 4s^2\ 3d^6$
14. F: $1s^2\ 2s^2\ 2p^5$
15. Mn: $1s^2\ 2s^2\ 2p^6\ 3s^2\ 3p^6\ 4s^2\ 3d^5$
16. Zn: $1s^2\ 2s^2\ 2p^6\ 3s^2\ 3p^6\ 4s^2\ 3d^{10}$
17. P: $1s^2\ 2s^2\ 2p^6\ 3s^2\ 3p^3$
18. Li: $1s^2\ 2s^1$
19. Sc: $1s^2\ 2s^2\ 2p^6\ 3s^2\ 3p^6\ 4s^2\ 3d^1$
20. He: $1s^2$

ECN Practice 2
1. N: $1s^2\ 2s^2\ 2p^3$
2. O: $1s^2\ 2s^2\ 2p^4$
3. Mg: $1s^2\ 2s^2\ 2p^6\ 3s^2$
4. Si: $1s^2\ 2s^2\ 2p^6\ 3s^2\ 3p^2$
5. F: $1s^2\ 2s^2\ 2p^5$
6. S: $1s^2\ 2s^2\ 2p^6\ 3s^2\ 3p^4$
7. Ne: $1s^2\ 2s^2\ 2p^6$
8. Mn: $1s^2\ 2s^2\ 2p^6\ 3s^2\ 3p^6\ 4s^2\ 3d^5$
9. Mg: $1s^2\ 2s^2\ 2p^6\ 3s^2$
10. Sr: $1s^2\ 2s^2\ 2p^6\ 3s^2\ 3p^6\ 4s^2\ 3d^{10}\ 4p^6\ 5s^2$
11. Bo: $1s^2\ \underline{2p^2\ 3p^1}$ 3 errors
12. Na_$1s^2\ 2s^2\ 2p–3s^5$ 3 errors
13. Ph: $1s^2\ 2s^2\ 2p^6\ 3s^3\ \underline{4s^2}$ 3+ errors
14. K: $1s^2\ 2s^2\ 2p^6\ 3s^2\ 3p^6\ 4s^1$ No errors
15. CA: $1s^2\ \ 2s^2\ 2p^6\ 3s^2\ 3p^5 4s^2\ \underline{3d^1}$ 3+ errors

Lesson 6 Test
1. C: $1s^2\ 2s^2\ 2p^2$
2. O: $1s^2\ 2s^2\ 2p^4$
3. Ne: $1s^2\ 2s^2\ 2p^6$
4. Al: $1s^2\ 2s^2\ 2p^6\ 3s^2\ 3p^1$
5. Ca: $1s^2\ 2s^2\ 2p^6\ 3s^2\ 3p^6\ 4s^2$
6. Cl: $1s^2\ 2s^2\ 2p^6\ 3s^2\ 3p^5$
7. Cu: $1s^2\ 2s^2\ 2p^6\ 3s^2\ 3p^6\ 4s^2\ 3d^9$
8. As: $1s^2\ 2s^2\ 2p^6\ 3s^2\ 3p^6\ 4s^2\ 3d^{10}4p^3$
9. Br: $1s^2\ 2s^2\ 2p^6\ 3s^2\ 3p^6\ 4s^2\ 3d^{10}4p^5$
10. Na: $1s^2\ 2s^2\ 2p^6\ 3s^1$

Lesson 7
Electron Dot Notation Practice
1. C: $1s^2\ 2s^2\ 2p^2$ 4 dots
2. B: $1s^2\ 2s^2\ 2p^1$ 3 dots
3. Cl: $1s^2\ 2s^2\ 2p^6\ 3s^2\ 3p^5$ 7 dots
4. Ne: $1s^2\ 2s^2\ 2p^6$ 8 dots
5. F: $1s^2\ 2s^2\ 2p^5$ 7 dots
6. Be: $1s^2\ 2s^2$ 2 dots
7. Na: $1s^2\ 2s^2\ 2p^6\ 3s^1$ 1 dot
8. Al: $1s^2\ 2s^2\ 2p^6\ 3s^2\ 3p^1$ 3 dots
9. Si: $1s^2\ 2s^2\ 2p^6\ 3s^2\ 3p^2$ 4 dots
10. K: $1s^2\ 2s^2\ 2p^6\ 3s^2\ 3p^6\ 4s^1$ 1 dot
11. Mg: $1s^2\ 2s^2\ 2p^6\ 3s^2$ 2 dots

12. Cr: $1s^2\ 2s^2\ 2p^6\ 3s^2\ 3p^6\ 4s^2\ 3d^4$ 2 dots
13. Ti: $1s^2\ 2s^2\ 2p^6\ 3s^2\ 3p^6\ 4s^2\ 3d^2$ 2 dots
14. Li: $1s^2\ 2s^1$ 1 dot
15. Mn: $1s^2\ 2s^2\ 2p^6\ 3s^2\ 3p^6\ 4s^2\ 3d^5$ 2 dots
16. V: $1s^2\ 2s^2\ 2p^6\ 3s^2\ 3p^6\ 4s^2\ 3d^3$ 2 dots
17. P: $1s^2\ 2s^2\ 2p^6\ 3s^2\ 3p^3$ 5 dots
18. As: $1s^2\ 2s^2\ 2p^6\ 3s^2\ 3p^6\ 4s^2\ 3d^{10}\ 4p^3$ 5 dots
19. Sc: $1s^2\ 2s^2\ 2p^6\ 3s^2\ 3p^6\ 4s^2\ 3d^1$ 2 dots
20. H: $1s^1$ 1 dot

Electron Dot Notation Practice 2

1. 8 dots
2. 3 dots
3. 7 dots
4. 5 dots
5. 2 dots
6. 6 dots
7. 1 dot
8. 3 dots
9. 7 dots
10. 1 dot
11. 2 dots
12. 2 dots
13. 2 dots
14. 2 dots
15. 2 dots
16. 2 dots
17. 4 dots
18. 6 dots
19. 8 dots
20. 2 dots

Lesson 7 Test

1. A
2. A
3. D
4. C
5. B
6. C
7. B
8. D
9. C
10. B

Lesson 8

Element Family Practice 1

1. 1 dot, sodium family
2. 6 dots, oxygen family
3. 2 dots, noble gas family
4. 1 dot, sodium family
5. 7 dots, halogen family
6. 2 dots, calcium family
7. 2 dots, calcium family
8. 1 dot, sodium family
9. 8 dots, noble gas family
10. 6 dots, oxygen family
11. 2 dots, calcium family
12. 7 dots, halogen family
13. 2 dots, calcium family
14. 7 dots, halogen family
15. 1 dot, sodium family
16. 7 dots, halogen family
17. 2 dots, calcium family

18. 8 dots, noble gas family
19. 8 dots, noble gas family
20. 1 dot, sodium family

Element Family Practice 2

1. 4 dots, carbon family
2. 2 dots, noble gas family
3. 6 dots, oxygen family
4. 8 dots, noble gas family
5. 2 dots, calcium family
6. 2 dots, calcium family
7. 7 dots, halogen family
8. 8 dots, noble gas family
9. 8 dots, noble gas family
10. 7 dots, halogen family
11. 1 dot, sodium family
12. 1 dot, sodium family
13. 1 dot, sodium family
14. 6 dots, oxygen family
15. 6 dots, oxygen family
16. 2 dots, calcium family
17. 7 dots, halogen family
18. 8 dots, noble gas family
19. 1 dot, sodium family

Lesson 8 Test

1. 1 dot, 1 valence electron, sodium family
2. 6 dots, 6 valence electrons, oxygen family
3. 2 dots, 2 valence electrons, calcium family
4. 8 dots, 8 valence electrons, noble gas family
5. 2 dots, 2 valence electrons, calcium family
6. 1 dot, 1 valence electron, sodium family
7. 2 dots, 2 valence electrons, calcium family
8. 7 dots, 7 valence electrons, halogen family
9. 1 dot, 1 valence electron, sodium family
10. 7 dots, 7 valence electrons, halogen family

Lesson 9

Lesson 9 Practice Page

Terms as they appear in order:
Valence
Sodium
2
Six
Seven
Noble gas
Helium
2
Ionization energy
High
Noble gas family
Non-reactive
Inert
Helium, neon, argon, krypton, xenon and radon
Low
React
Reactive
Sodium
Hydrogen, lithium, sodium, potassium, rubidium, cesium and francium
Sodium
Water
Hydrogen
Reactivity
Ionization energy
Families

Lesson 9 Test

1. True
2. False
3. False
4. False
5. True
6. False
7. False
8. True
9. True
10. False

Bonus: helium, neon, argon, krypton, xenon and radon.

Lesson 10

Lesson 10 Practice Page-Atomic Size

1. Na
2. Na
3. K
4. Cr
5. Ga
6. N
7. Xe
8. Os
9. Ca
10. Cu
11. Fr
12. Ni
13. Te
14. As
15. Tc
16. Mg
17. Rn
18. K
19. Ca
20. Al

Lesson 10 Test

1. C
2. A
3. Cesium
4. Calcium
5. Selenium
6. Potassium
7. Mercury
8. Iodine
9. Zirconium
10. Iron

Lesson 11

Ion Formation Practice

1. Sodium, 11, 1, loses, 1, sodium cation
2. Sodium, 3, 1, loses, 1, lithium cation
3. Sodium, 19, loses, 1, potassium cation
4. Calcium, 20, 2, loses, 2, calcium cation
5. Calcium, 56, 2, loses, 2, barium cation
6. Sodium, 1, 1, loses, 1, hydrogen cation
7. Halogen, 17, 7, gains, 1, chloride
8. Oxygen, 8, 6, gains 2, oxide
9. Halogen, 53, 7, gains 1, iodide
10. Sodium, 55, 1, loses, 1, cesium cation
11. Halogen, 9, 7, gains, 1, fluoride
12. Oxygen, 16, 6, gains, 2, sulfide

13. Oxygen, 34, 6, gains, 2, selenide
14. Oxygen, 84, 6, gains, 2, polonide
15. Sodium, 87, 1, loses, 1, francium cation
16. Calcium, 12, 2, loses, 2, magnesium cation
17. Oxygen, 52, 6, gains, 2, telluride
18. Halogen, 85, 7, gains, 1, astatide
19. Calcium, 38, 2, loses 2, strontium cation
20. Noble gas, 18, 8, neither gains nor loses!

Lesson 11 Test—Ionization

1. halogen, 17, 7, gains, 1, chloride
2. Sodium, 3, 1, loses, 1, lithium cation
3. Calcium, 20, 2, loses, 2, calcium cation
4. Halogen, 53, 7, gains, 1, iodide
5. Sodium, 11, 1, loses, 1, sodium cation
6. Sodium, 1, 1, loses, 1, hydrogen cation
7. Calcium, 12, 2, loses, 2, magnesium cation
8. Oxygen, 16, 6, gains, 2, sulfide
9. Halogen, 9, 7, gains, 1, fluoride
10. Sodium, 55, 1, loses, 1, cesium cation

Lesson 12

Lesson 12—Ion Formation Practice

1. 1, loses, 1, Na^{+1} Sodium cation
2. 1, loses, 1, Li^{+1} Lithium cation
3. 1, loses, 1, K^{+1} Potassium cation
4. 2, loses, 2, Ca^{+2} Calcium cation
5. 2, loses, 2, Ba^{+2} Barium cation
6. 1, loses, 1, H^{+1} Hydrogen cation
7. 7, gains, 1, Cl^{-1} Chloride

8. 6, gains, 2, O^{-2} Oxide
9. 7, gains, 1, I^{-1} Iodide
10. 1, loses, 1, Cs^{+1} Cesium cation
11. 7, gains, 1, F^{-1} Fluoride
12. 6, gains, 2, S^{-2} Sulfide
13. 6, gains, 2, Se^{-2} Selenide
14. 6, gains, 2, Po^{-2} Polonide
15. 1, loses, 1, Fr^{+1} Francium cation
16. 2, loses, 2, Mg^{+2} Magnesium cation
17. 6, gains, 2, Te^{-2} Telluride
18. 7, gains, 1, At^{-1} Astatide
19. 2, loses, 2, Sr^{+2} Strontium cation
20. 1, loses, 1, Rb^{+1} Rubidium cation

Lesson 12 Ion Practice 2

1. Cl^{-1} Anion
2. F^{-1} Anion
3. Na^{+1} Cation
4. I^{-1} Anion
5. Mg^{+2} Cation
6. Ca^{+2} Cation
7. Sr^{+2} Cation
8. O^{-2} Anion
9. S^{-2} Anion
10. H^{+1} Cation
11. Be^{+2} Cation
12. K^{+1} Cation
13. Se^{-2} Anion
14. Rb^{+1} Cation
15. Li^{+1} Cation

Lesson 12 Test

1. O^{-2}

2. Li^{+1}
3. Se^{-2}
4. K^{+1}
5. Po^{-2}
6. F^{-1}
7. Fr^{+1}
8. Br^{-1}
9. Mg^{+2}
10. At^{-1}
11. Sr^{+2}
12. Ba^{+2}
13. H^{+1}
14. S^{-2}
15. Na^{+1}
16. Te^{-2}
17. Rb^{+1}
18. Cs^{+1}
19. Cl^{-1}
20. Be^{+2}
21. I^{-1}
22. Ca^{+2}
23. Ra^{+2}

Lesson 13

Writing Simple Chemical Formulas-1

1. $Na^{+1}{}_1F^{-1}{}_1$
2. $K^{+1}{}_1Cl^{-1}{}_1$
3. $Li^{+1}{}_1Br^{-1}{}_1$
4. $H^{+1}{}_1Cl^{-1}{}_1$
5. $Mg^{+2}{}_1O^{-2}{}_1$
6. $Ca^{+2}{}_1S^{-2}{}_1$
7. $Be^{+2}{}_1O^{-2}{}_1$
8. $K^{+1}{}_1I^{-1}{}_1$
9. $Cs^{+1}{}_1Cl^{-1}{}_1$
10. $Na^{+1}{}_1Br^{-1}{}_1$

Writing Simple Chemical Formulas-2

1. $Na^1{}_1I^{-1}{}_1$
2. $K^{+1}{}_1Cl^{-1}{}_1$
3. $Li^{+1}{}_2O^{-2}{}_1$
4. $H^{+1}{}_2S^{-2}{}_1$
5. $Mg^{+2}{}_1Br^{-1}{}_2$
6. $Ca^{+2}{}_1S^{-2}{}_1$
7. $Be^{+2}{}_1Po^{-2}{}_1$
8. $Sr^{+2}{}_1I^{-1}{}_2$
9. $Cs^{+1}{}_1Cl^{-1}{}_1$
10. $Na^{+1}{}_2Se^{-2}{}_1$

Lesson 13 Test

1. $K^{+1}{}_1F^{-1}{}_1$
2. $Na^{+1}{}_1Cl^{-1}{}_1$
3. $Li^{+1}{}_2O^{-2}{}_1$
4. $H_2{}^{+1}Se^{-2}{}_1$
5. $Mg^{+2}{}_1O^{-2}{}_1$
6. $Ba^{+2}{}_1S^{-2}{}_1$
7. $Be^{+2}{}_1O^{-2}{}_1$
8. $K^{+1}{}_1I^{-1}{}_1$
9. $Cs^{+1}{}_1Cl^{-1}{}_1$
10. $Mg^{+2}{}_1Br^{-1}{}_2$

Lesson 14

Ion Practice 1

1. Ca^{+2}

2. Na^{+1}
3. F^{-1}
4. Cl^{-1}
5. $(ClO_1)^{-1}$
6. $(ClO_2)^{-1}$
7. $(ClO_4)^{-1}$
8. $(SO_3)^{-2}$
9. $(SO_4)^{-2}$
10. $(NO_3)^{-1}$
11. $(NO_2)^{-1}$
12. $(OH)^{-1}$
13. Zn^{+2}
14. H^{+1}
15. $(CrO_4)^{-2}$
16. $(Cr_2O_7)^{-2}$
17. Ag^{+1}
18. Ni^{+2}
19. Acetate
20. Iodide
21. Nitrite
22. Cyanide
23. Nickel
24. Tin (II)
25. Silver cation
26. Sulfide
27. Tin (IV)
28. Hypochlorite
29. Sulfate
30. Chlorate
31. Perchlorate
32. Chlorite
33. Hypochlorite
34. Hydroxide
35. Lithium cation
36. Barium cation

Ion Practice 2

1. $(SO_4)^{-2}$
2. $(SO_3)^{-2}$
3. O^{-2}
4. $(ClO_4)^{-1}$
5. I^{-1}
6. Li^{+1}
7. Na^{+1}
8. Pb^{+2}
9. $(PO_4)^{-3}$
10. S^{-2}
11. $(ClO_1)^{-1}$
12. $(NH_4)^{+1}$
13. Ca^{+2}
14. K^{+1}
15. Ba^{+2}
16. $(OH)^{-1}$
17. Chlorate
18. Bromide
19. Mercury (II)
20. Nitrate
21. Phosphate
22. Hydroxide
23. Perchlorate
24. Permanganate
25. Hydrogen cation
26. Chlorite
27. Chloride
28. Sulfite
29. Chromate
30. Ammonium
31. Peroxide
32. Sodium cation

Ion Practice 3

1. $(ClO_2)^{-1}$
2. Na^{+1}
3. $(SO_3)^{-2}$
4. Cl^{-1}
5. $(NO_3)^{-1}$
6. Ca^{+2}
7. $(ClO_4)^{-1}$
8. Zn^{+2}
9. $(SO_4)^{-2}$
10. $(ClO_1)^{-1}$
11. $(NO_2)^{-1}$
12. $(OH)^{-1}$
13. F^{-1}
14. H^{+1}
15. Ni^{+2}
16. $(Cr_2O_7)^{-2}$
17. Ag^{+1}
18. $(CrO_4)^{-2}$
19. Tin (IV)
20. Iodide
21. Hypochlorite
22. Cyanide
23. Sulfate
24. Tin (II)
25. Silver cation
26. Sulfide
27. Acetate
28. Hypochlorite
29. Nickel
30. Chlorate
31. Perchlorate
32. Sodium cation
33. Nitrite
34. Hydroxide
35. Chlorite
36. Strontium cation

Lesson 14 Test

1. Na^{+1}
2. $(SO_3)^{-2}$
3. $(PO_4)^{-3}$
4. $(ClO_4)^{-1}$
5. I^{-1}
6. $(ClO_3)^{-1}$
7. $(SO_4)^{-2}$
8. Pb^{+4}
9. O^{-2}
10. S^{-2}
11. $(ClO_1)^{-1}$
12. $(NH_4)^{+1}$
13. $(Cr_2O_7)^{-2}$
14. $(CO_3)^{-2}$
15. $(O_2)^{-2}$
16. $(OH)^{-1}$
17. Chlorate
18. Bromide
19. Mercury (II)
20. Nitrate
21. Phosphate
22. Hydroxide
23. Perchlorate
24. Permanganate
25. Hydrogen cation
26. Chlorite
27. Chloride
28. Sulfite

29. Chromate
30. Ammonium
31. Peroxide
32. Sodium cation

Lesson 15

Compound Writing Practice

1. $Na_1^{+1}Cl_1^{-1}$
2. $K_1^{+1}(NO_3)_1^{-1}$
3. $Li_1^{+1}Cl_1^{-1}$
4. $Ba_1^{+2}(SO_3)_1^{-2}$
5. $Ca_1^{+2}(CO_3)_1^{-2}$
6. $Sr_1^{+2}O_1^{-2}$
7. $Sn_1^{+4}(SO_4)_2^{-2}$
8. $H_1^{+1}(ClO_3)_1^{-1}$
9. $K_1^{+1}(ClO_4)_1^{-1}$
10. $Al_1^{+3}(C_2H_3O_2)_3^{-1}$
11. $Mg_1^{+2}(SO_3)_1^{-2}$
12. $Hg_1^{+2}Br_2^{-1}$
13. $Na_2^{+1}(Cr_2O_7)_1^{-2}$
14. $Sr_1^{+2}I_2^{-1}$
15. $(NH_4)_2^{+1}(Cr_2O_7)_1^{-2}$
16. $K_1^{+1}Cl_1^{-1}$
17. $Cr_1^{+3}(ClO_4)_3^{-1}$
18. $Ca_1^{+2}(CN)_2^{-1}$
19. $Ba_1^{+2}(ClO_2)_2^{-1}$
20. $(NH_4)_1^{+1}Cl_1^{-1}$
21. $Ba_1^{+2}(OH)_2^{-1}$
22. $Ca_1^{+2}(NO_2)_2^{-1}$
23. $Cs_2^{+1}(SO_4)_1^{-2}$
24. $Ni_1^{+2}(NO_3)_2^{-1}$
25. $Ca_1^{+2}O_1^{-2}$
26. $Na_1^{+1}Br_1^{-1}$
27. $Ag_2^{+1}(CrO_4)_1^{-2}$
28. $Cu_1^{+2}F_2^{-1}$
29. $K_1^{+1}(MnO_4)_1^{-1}$
30. $Li_2^{+1}(CO_3)_1^{-2}$
31. $Ni_1^{+2}(CN)_2^{-1}$
32. $Pb_1^{+2}(ClO_1)_2^{-1}$
33. $Zn_1^{+2}(ClO_2)_2^{-1}$
34. $H_2^{+1}(O_2)_1^{-2}$
35. $Cu_2^{+1}(SO_3)_1^{-2}$
36. $(H_3O)_2^{+1}S_1^{-2}$
37. $Ni_3^{+2}(PO_4)_2^{-3}$
38. $Hg_1^{+2}(CO_3)_1^{-2}$
39. $Sn_1^{+4}(SO_4)_2^{-2}$
40. $K_1^{+1}(OH)_1^{-1}$

Lesson 15 Test

1. $Ba_1^{+2}(OH)_2^{-1}$
2. $Ca_1^{+2}(NO_3)_2^{-1}$
3. $(NH_4)_2^{+1}(SO_4)_1^{-2}$
4. $Hg_1^{+2}(ClO_2)_2^{-1}$
5. $Al_1^{+3}(PO_4)_1^{-3}$
6. $Ag_2^{+1}O_1^{-2}$
7. $Cu_1^{+1}(CN)_1^{-1}$
8. $K_2^{+1}(SO_3)_1^{-2}$
9. $(H_3O)_1^{+1}(NO_2)_1^{-1}$
10. $H_2^{+1}(O_2)_1^{-2}$
11. $Ca_1^{+2}(SO_3)_1^{-2}$
12. $Sr_1^{+2}(CO_3)_1^{-2}$
13. $Pb_1^{+2}(ClO_1)_2^{-1}$
14. $Cr_1^{+3}(C_2H_3O_2)_3^{-1}$
15. $K_1^{+1}(MnO_4)_1^{-1}$
16. $Mg_1^{+2}(ClO_3)_2^{-1}$
17. $Ni_1^{+2}S_1^{-2}$
18. $Li_2^{+1}(CrO_4)_1^{-2}$
19. $(NH_4)_2^{+1}(Cr_2O_7)_1^{-2}$
20. $Al_1^{+3}(ClO_4)_3^{-1}$
21. Sodium nitrate
22. Barium carbonate
23. Potassium permanganate
24. Magnesium sulfate
25. Nickel chlorate
26. Lead (II) chloride
27. Zinc perchlorate
28. Calcium cyanide
29. Ammonium oxide
30. Aluminum hydroxide

Friendly Chemistry

Name_____ Date_____

Friendly Chemistry

Lesson 16: Making Mole to Gram Conversions

Below are mole amounts of elements you need to get for your teacher. How many grams of each element do you need to weigh-out? Use your periodic table and calculator!

Moles Needed	Grams I need to weigh-out	Moles Needed	Grams I need to weigh-out
1. 2 moles of sodium	2 x 23 g/mole = 46 g	11. 5 moles of carbon	5 x 12g/m = 60 g
2. 10 moles of beryllium	10 x 9g/m = 90 g	12. 4.5 moles of lithium	4.5 x 7g/m = 31.5g
3. 13 moles of boron	13 x 11g/m = 143 g	13. 7.5 moles of lead	7.5 x 207g/m = 1552.5 g
4. 0.5 moles of cesium	0.5 x 133g/m = 66.5 g	14. 45 moles of barium	45 x 137g/m = 6165 g
5. 0.25 moles of helium	0.25 x 4 g/m = 1 g	15. 14.75 moles of oxygen	14.75 x 16 g/m = 236 g
6. 4.56 moles of calcium	4.56 x 40g/m = 182.4 g	16. 34 moles of silicon	34 x 28g/m = 952 g
7. 24.75 moles of aluminum	24.75 x 27g/m = 668.25 g	17. 23 moles of vanadium	23 x 51g/m = 1173g
8. 72 moles magnesium	72 x 24g/m = 1728 g	18. 0.05 moles of gold	.05 x 197g/m = 9.85g
9. 34.7 moles of manganese	34.7 x 55g/m = 1908.5g	19. 4343.4 moles of sulfur	4343.4 x 32g/m = 138,988.8g
10. 0.15 moles of fluorine	0.15 x 19g/m = 2.85g	20. 1 mole of nitrogen (a little easier being the last one!)	1 x 14g/m = 14 g

Friendly Chemistry

Name_____ Date_____

Friendly Chemistry

Lesson 16: More Gram to Mole Conversion Practice

Below are problems that ask you to make gram to mole and mole to gram conversions. Take your time and work carefully. Ask questions if you're not sure what to do!

1. Mickey needed to get 5.5 moles of calcium from the store room. How many grams should Mickey get?

    5.5 m x 40g/m = ***220 grams Ca.***

2. Minnie was doing a chemical reaction which called for 4 moles of sodium metal. If she had a container which contained 100 grams of sodium metal and it was full, would she have enough? Support your answer with your calculations.

    4 m x 23g/m = 92 grams
    Yes, 100 grams would be adequate.

3. Pluto had 5 moles of lithium. Yosemite Sam had 5 moles of carbon. Who had more atoms of their elements? Support your answer with calculations.

    Each has the same number of moles, therefore ***each has the same number of atoms.***

4. Fred had a recipe for making calcium carbonate. It called for 5 moles of carbon. If Barney had 55 grams of carbon, would he have enough to give Fred for the recipe? Support your answer with calculations.

    5 m x 12 g/m = 60 grams of carbon; ***Barney does not have enough.***

5. Daffy and Donald were looking at some labels on some chemicals. On one container it stated that 50 moles of magnesium were present in the container when new, however, the container had been partially used. If Daffy weighed the magnesium that remained the container and found it was 350 grams, how many moles were used?

50 m x 24g/m = 1200 grams in the full container.
1200 g—350 g = 850 grams were used.
850 g / 24g/mole = **35.4 moles were used.**

6. Sleepy told Dopey to get 56 moles of lead to make some fishing weights. Dopey returned with 11.6 kg of lead. Did he get enough to make the fishing weights? Support your answer with calculations.

56 m x 207g/mole = 11,592 grams were needed.

Dopey's 11.6 kg would be adequate (1000 g = 1 kilogram)

7. Hank and Drover were out chasing cows one day and the pickup ran out of gas. Drover had learned in his latest edition of Popular Science that corn could be make into ethanol which could be used like gas. In order for the recipe to work correctly, Drover needed 90 moles of oxygen gas. How many grams of oxygen should he get?

90 moles x 16 grams/mole = **1440 grams oxygen**

Friendly Chemistry

NAME_____ DATE_____
FRIENDLY CHEMISTRY

Lesson 16 Test

Read each problem carefully. Show your work if you make calculations. Check over your answers when you are done!

1. Toby had 10 moles of calcium. How many **grams** of calcium did he have?

    One mole of calcium has a mass of 40 grams.
    *10 moles x 40 grams per mole = **400 grams**.*

Grams of calcium: _____

2. Patty had 22 moles of barium. Sara had 22 moles of copper. Who had more **atoms** of their element?

    *As they each had the same number of moles, they would have the **same number of atoms.***

Who had more? _____

3. Maurice needed 5 moles of carbon for his lab activity. In the unused bottle of carbon he had on his shelf the label read 50 grams. Would he have enough carbon if he used this bottle? Show proof of your answer.

Yes _____   No ___X_____

Why or why not? *One mole of carbon has a mass of 12 grams. 5 moles would be equal to 60 grams of carbon. If Maurice had 50 grams, **that amount would not be enough.***

4. Tonette had 420 grams of zinc. How many moles of zinc did she have?

    One mole of zinc has a mass of 65 grams.
    *420 grams / 65 grams per mole = **6.46 moles of Zn**.*

Moles of zinc: _____

Name_____ Date_____
Friendly Chemistry
        Lesson 17: Finding Formula Weights Practice –1

Find the formula weights for the following compounds.

1. Sodium oxide

Na_2O_1
Na: 2 x 23 g = 46 g
O: 1 x 16 g = 16 g

Formula weight: _____62 g_____

2. Barium fluoride

Ba_1F_2
Ba: 1 x 137g = 137 g
F: 2 x 19g = 38 g

Formula weight: _____175 g_____

3. Aluminum sulfide

Al_2S_3
Al: 2 x 27g = 54g
S: 3 x 32 g = 96 g

Formula weight: ____150 g_____

4. Nickel carbonate

$Ni(CO_3)$
Ni: 1 x 59 g = 59 g
C: 1 x 12g = 12 g
O: 3 x 16g = 48 g

Formula weight: _____119 g_____

5. Calcium chlorate
$Ca(ClO_3)_2$
Ca: 1 x 40 g = 40 g
Cl: 2 x 35 g = 70 g
O: 6 x 16 g = 96 g
Formula weight: _____206 g_____

6. Barium permanganate
$Ba(MnO_4)_2$
Ba: 1 x 137g = 137g
Mn: 2 x 54g = 108g
O: 8 x 16g = 128 g
Formula weight: _____373 g_____

7. Zinc hydroxide
$Zn(OH)_2$
Zn: 1 x 65g = 65 g
O: 2 x 16g = 32 g
H: 2 x 1 g = 2 g
Formula weight: _____99g_____

8. Potassium nitrate
$K(NO_3)$
K: 1 x 39g = 39g
N: 1 x 14g = 14 g
O: 3 x 16g = 48g
Formula weight: _____101 g_____

9. Sodium phosphate
$Na_3(PO_4)$
Na: 3 x 23 g = 69g
P: 1 x 31g = 31g
O: 4 x 16g = 64 g
Formula weight: _____164 g_____

10. Lithium sulfite
$Li_2(SO_3)$
Li: 2 x 7g = 14 g
S: 1 x 32g = 32 g
O: 3 x 16 g = 48 g
Formula weight: _____94 g_____

11. Calcium acetate
$Ca(C_2H_3O_2)_2$
Ca: 1 x 40g = 40 g
C: 4 x 12g = 48 g
H: 6 x 1 g = 6 g
O: 4 x 16g = 64 g
Formula weight: _____158 g_____

12. Chromium perchlorate $Cr(ClO_4)_3$
Cr: 1 x 52g =52 g   Cl: 3 x 35g = 105g   O: 12 x 16g = 192 g
Formula weight: _____349 g_____

Name_____ Date_____

Friendly Chemistry

Lesson 17: Formula Weight Practice –2

1. Joel needed to prepare a mole of potassium oxide. How many grams should be get from the stock container?

K_2O_1
K: 2 x 39g = 78 g
O: 1 x 16 g = 16 g
Total: 94 grams/mole, therefore Joel needs to get **94 grams**.

2. Mary was asked to prepare 3 moles of sodium chloride for a lab activity. How many grams should she get?

NaCl
Na: 1 x 23 g = 23 g
Cl: 1 x 35 g = 35 g
Total: 58 g   Mary needs 3 moles, so 3 x 58g = **174 g**

3. Frank had 3 moles of lead (II) oxide. How many grams of this compound did he have?

PbO
Pb: 1 x 207 g = 207 g
O: 1 x 16 g = 16 g
Total: 223 g   Frank has three moles, so 3 x 223 g = **669 g**

4. Sarah had 10 moles of hydrogen phosphate. How many grams of this compound did she have?

$H_3(PO_4)$
H: 3 x 1g = 3 g
P: 1 x 31 g = 31 g
O: 4 x 16 g = 64 g
Total: 98 g. Sarah had 10 moles, so 10 x 98g = **980 g**

5. Horace had 12 moles of carbon. Julie had 144 grams of carbon. Who had the most carbon?

Horace had 12 moles. One mole of carbon = 12 g. So, 12 x 12 g = 144 g
Julie had 144 g.
They had the same amount of carbon: 144 g.

6. Francis was conducting a lab exercise which required she use 9 moles of iron (III) sulfate. She looked in the chemical closet and found she had a full container of the compound. The label said there was 500 grams in the bottle. Did she have enough? Show your work as proof of your answer.

$Fe_2(SO_4)_3$
Fe: 2 x 56 g = 112 g
S: 3 x 32 g = 96 g
O: 12 x 16 g = 192 g
Total: 400 grams
Francis needed 9 moles, so 9 x 400g = 3600 grams. **So, no, Francis would not have enough in her container.**

7. Joey was given 1000 grams of calcium carbonate (limestone). How many moles did he have?

$Ca(CO_3)$
Ca: 1 x 40 g = 40 g
C: 1 x 12 g = 12 g
O: 3 x 16 g = 48 g
Total: 100 g

Joey had 1000 grams, therefore 1000g / 100g/mole = **10 moles $Ca(CO_3)$**

8. Terry had two containers of copper (I) sulfite. One said it had 3.5 moles and the second container's label said it contained 4.75 moles of the compound. How many grams of copper (I) sulfite did Terry have?

$Cu_2(SO_3)$
Cu: 2 x 64 g = 128 g
S: 1 x 32 g = 32 g
O: 3 x 16 g = 48 g
Total: 208 g per mole.

Terry had 3.5 moles plus 4.75 moles for a total of 8.25 moles.
So, 8.25 x 208 g/mole = **1716 grams $Cu_2(SO_3)$**

NAME_____ DATE_____

FRIENDLY CHEMISTRY

Lesson 17 Test
Finding Formula Weights

Find the formula weight of each compound listed below. Show your work!

---

1. Sodium chloride
Na: 1 x 23 g = 23 g
Cl: 1 x 35 g = 35 g
Formula weight = _____58 g_____

---

2. Barium oxide
$Ba^{+2}(O)^{-2}$ Ba: 1 x 137 g = 137 g
           O: 1 x 16 g = 16 g
Formula weight = _____153 g_____

---

3. Calcium sulfate $Ca(SO_4)$
Ca: 1 x 40 g = 40 g
S: 1 x 32 g = 32 g   O: 4 x 16 g = 64 g
Formula weight = _____136 g_____

---

4. Magnesium phosphate $Mg_3(PO_4)_2$
Mg: 3 x 24 g = 72 g
P: 2 x 31 g = 62 g   O: 8 x 16 g = 128 g
Formula weight = _____262 g_____

---

5. Zinc nitrate $Zn(NO_3)_2$
Zn: 1 x 65 g = 65 g
N: 2 x 14 g = 28 g   O: 6 x 16 g = 96 g
Formula weight = _____189 g_____

---

6. Lithium carbonate $Li_2(CO_3)$
Li: 2 x 7 g = 14 g
C: 1 x 12 = 12   O: 3 x 16 = 48 g
Formula weight = _____74 g_____

---

7. Copper (II) chlorite $Cu(ClO_2)_2$
Cu: 1 x 64 g = 64 g
Cl: 2 x 35 g = 70 g   O: 4 x 16g = 64 g
Formula weight = _____198 g_____

---

8. Ammonium sulfide $(NH_4)_2S$
N: 2 x 14g = 28 g
H: 8 x 1 = 8 g   S: 1 x 32g = 32 g
Formula weight = _____68 g_____

---

9. Aluminum hydroxide $Al(OH)_3$
Al: 1 x 27 g = 27 g
O: 3 x 16 = 48 g   H: 3 x 1 g = 3 g
Formula weight = _____78 g_____

---

10. Lead (IV) hypochlorite $Pb(ClO)_4$
Pb: 1 x 207 g = 207 g
Cl: 4 x 35 = 140 g   O: 4 x 16 = 64 g
Formula weight = _____411 g_____

Name_____ Date_____

Friendly Chemistry

Lesson 18
Finding Percent Composition of Compounds –1

Find the percent composition of each compound below.

---

1. hydrogen chloride
HCl
H: $1 \times 1\,g = 1\,g$
Cl: $1 \times 35\,g = 35\,g$

Formula weight: ____36g_____   Percent Composition: _3% H 97% Cl_____

---

2. sodium carbonate
$Na_2(CO_3)$
Na: $2 \times 23\,g = 46\,g$
C: $1 \times 12\,g = 12\,g$
O: $3 \times 16\,g = 48\,g$

Formula weight: ____106 g____   Percent Composition: _43% Na 11% C 45% O__

---

3. magnesium sulfate
$Mg(SO_4)$
Mg: $1 \times 24\,g = 24\,g$
S: $1 \times 32\,g = 32\,g$
O: $4 \times 16\,g = 64\,g$

Formula weight: _120 g_____   Percent Composition: __20% Mg 27% S 53% O_

---

4. chromium nitrate
$Cr(NO_3)_3$
Cr: $1 \times 52\,g = 52\,g$
N: $3 \times 14\,g = 42\,g$
O: $9 \times 16\,g = 144\,g$

Formula weight: ___238 g_____   Percent Composition: _21% Cr 18% N 61% O_

---

5. zinc acetate
$Zn(C_2H_3O_2)_2$
Zn: $1 \times 65\,g = 65\,g$
C: $4 \times 12g = 48\,g$
H: $6 \times 1\,g = 6\,g$
O: $4 \times 16\,g = 64\,g$
Formula weight: ___183g_____   Percent Composition: __35% Zn 26% C 3% H 35% O_

6. magnesium chlorate
$Mg(ClO_3)_2$
Mg: 1 x 24g = 24g
Cl: 2 x 35g = 70g
O: 6 x 16g = 96g

Formula weight: ___190g___   Percent Composition: ___13% Mg 37% Cl 51% O___

7. potassium nitrite
$K(NO_2)$
K: 1 x 39g = 39g
N: 1 x 14g = 14g
O: 2 x 16g = 32g

Formula weight: ___85 g___   Percent Composition: ___46% K 16% N 38% O___

8. aluminum phosphate

$Al(PO_4)$
Al: 1 x 27g = 27g
P: 1 x 31g = 31g
O: 4 x 16g = 64g

Formula weight: ___122g___   Percent Composition: ___21% Al 26% P 53% O___

9. calcium chloride
$CaCl_2$
Ca: 1 x 40g = 40g
Cl: 2 x 35g = 70 g

Formula weight: ___110 g___   Percent Composition: ___36% Ca 64% Cl___

10. ammonium chromate
$(NH_4)_2(CrO_4)$
N: 2 x 14g = 28g
H: 8 x 1g = 8g
Cr: 1 x 52g = 52g
O: 4 x 16g = 64g

Formula weight: ___152 g___   Percent Composition: 18% N 5% H 34% Cr 42% O

Friendly Chemistry

Name_____ Date_____

Friendly Chemistry

Finding Percent Composition of Compounds –2

Find the percent composition of each compound below.

---

1. Magnesium hydroxide
$Mg(OH)_2$
Mg: 1 x 24 g = 24g
O: 2 x 16 g = 32 g
H: 2 x 1 g = 2 g

Formula weight: ___58g___   Percent Composition: __41% Mg 55% O 3% H__

---

2. Barium acetate
$Ba(C_2H_3O_2)_2$
Ba: 1 x 137 g = 137g
C: 4 x 12 g = 48g
H: 6 x 1g = 6 g
O: 4 x 16g = 64g
Formula weight: __255 g_   Percent Composition: _54% Ba 19%C 2% H 25% O

---

3. Magnesium sulfite
$Mg(SO_3)$
Mg: 1 x 24g = 24g
S: 1 x 32g = 32g
O: 3 x 16g = 48g

Formula weight: _104g_____   Percent Composition: _23% Mg 31% S 46% O_

---

4. Aluminum nitrite
$Al(NO_2)_3$
Al: 1 x 27g = 27g
N: 3 x 14g = 42g
O: 6 x 16g = 96g

Formula weight: __165 g__   Percent Composition: 16% Al 26% N 59% O_

---

5. Zinc carbonate
$Zn(CO_3)$
Zn: 1 x 65g = 65g
C: 1 x 12g = 12 g
O: 3 x 16g = 48 g

Formula weight: ___125 g_   Percent Composition: _52% Zn 10% C 38% O_

6. Calcium hypochlorite
$Ca(ClO_1)_2$
Ca: 1 x 40g = 40g
Cl: 2 x 35g = 70g
O: 2 x 16g = 32g

Formula weight: __142g__   Percent Composition: __28% Ca 49% Cl 23% O__

7. Hydrogen fluoride
HF
H: 1 x 1g = 1g
F: 1 x 19g = 19g

Formula weight: __20g__   Percent Composition: __5% H 95% F__

8. Sodium phosphate
$Na_3(PO_4)_1$
Na: 3 x 23 g = 69g
P: 1 x 31g = 31g
O: 4 x 16 g = 64g

Formula weight: __164 g__   Percent Composition: __42% Na 19% P 39% O__

9. Lithium chloride
LiCl
Li: 1 x 7g = 7g
Cl: 1 x 35g = 35g

Formula weight: __42 g__   Percent Composition: __17% Li 83% Cl__

10. Ammonium cyanide
$(NH_4)(CN)$
N: 2 x 14g = 28g
H: 4 x 1 g = 4g
C: 1 x 12g = 12g

Formula weight: __44g__   Percent Composition: __64% N 9% H 27% C__

Friendly Chemistry

Name_____ Date_____

Friendly Chemistry

Lesson 18 Test
Finding Percent Composition of Compounds

Find the percent composition of each compound below.

---

1. Barium chloride
$BaCl_2$
Ba: 1 x 137 g = 137 g; 137 / 207 = 66%
Cl: 2 x 35 g = 70 g; 70/ 207 = 34%
          207 g

Formula weight: _____   Percent Composition: _____

---

2. Sodium carbonate
$Na_2(CO_3)$
Na: 2 x 23 g = 46 g   46/106 = 43%
C: 1 x 12 = 12 g   12/206 = 11%
O: 3 x 16 g = 48 g   48/206 = 45%
          106 g

Formula weight: _____   Percent Composition: _____

---

3. Magnesium sulfite
$Mg(SO_3)$
Mg: 1 x 24 g = 24 g   24/104 = 23%
S: 1 x 32 g = 32 g   32/104 = 31%
O: 3 x 16 g = 48 g   48/104= 46%
          104 g

Formula weight: _____   Percent Composition: _____

---

4. Aluminum nitrite
$Al(NO_2)_3$
Al: 1 x 27 g = 27 g   16%
N: 3 x 14 g = 42 g   26%
O: 6 x 16 g = 96 g   59%
          165 g

Formula weight: _____   Percent Composition: _____

---

5. Lead (II) acetate
$Pb(C_2H_3O_2)_2$
Pb: 1 x 207 g = 207 g 64%
C: 4 x 12 = 48 g   15%
H: 6 x 1 g = 6 g 2%
O: 4 x 16 g = 64 g   20%

Formula weight: ___325 g___   Percent Composition: _____

Friendly Chemistry

Name_____ Date_____
Friendly Chemistry

Lesson 19
Finding Empirical Formulas –1

Below are several analyses of unknown chemical compounds. Find the empirical formula for each compound. Then write the name of that compound in the appropriate space.

1. Analysis: 15% fluorine, 85% silver

F: 15% x 100g = 15 g/19 g per mole = 0.78 moles
Ag: 85% x 100 g = 85 g / 108 g per mole = 0.78 moles

Empirical formula: ___Ag_1F_1___ Name: Silver Fluoride

2. Analysis: 2.77% hydrogen and 97.3% chlorine

H: 2.77% x 100g = 2.77g / 1g/m = 2.77 m
Cl: 97.3% x 100g = 97.3g / 35g/m = 2.78 m

$H_{\frac{2.77}{2.77}} Cl_{\frac{2.78}{2.77}} \rightarrow H_1Cl_1$

Empirical formula: ___H_1Cl_1___ Name: __Hydrogen Chloride__

3. Analysis: 24.58% potassium, 34.81% manganese, 40.5% oxygen

K: 24.5% x 100g = 24.5g / 39g/m = 0.63 m
Mn: 34.81% x 100g = 34.81g / 55g/m = 0.63 m
O: 40.5% x 100g = 40.5g / 16g/m = 2.53 m

$K_{\frac{0.63}{0.63}} Mn_{\frac{0.63}{0.63}} O_{\frac{2.53}{0.63}}$

$K_1^{+1}(Mn_1O_4)^{-1}$

Empirical formula ___$K(MnO_4)$___ Name: __Potassium Permanganate__

4. Analysis: 9.66% nitrogen, 87.6% iodine, 2.79% hydrogen

N: 9.66% x 100g = 9.66g / 14g/m = 0.69 m
I: 87.6% x 100g = 87.6g / 127g/m = 0.69 m
H: 2.79% x 100g = 2.79g / 1g/m = 2.79 m

$N_{\frac{0.69}{0.69}} I_{\frac{0.69}{0.69}} H_{\frac{2.79}{0.69}}$

$N_1I_1H_4$

$\rightarrow (NH_4)_1^{+1} I_1^{-1}$

Empirical formula: ___$(NH_4)_1I_1$___ Name: ___Ammonium iodide___

Friendly Chemistry

Wait! There's more on the flip-side!!

5. Analysis: 60.7% chlorine, 39.3% sodium

Cl: 60.7% × 100g = 60.7g / 35g/m = 1.7 m
Na: 39.3% × 100g = 39.3g / 23g/m = 1.7 m

$Na_{1.7} Cl_{1.7}$
$Na_1^{+1} Cl_1^{-1}$

Empirical formula: _____NaCl_____ Name: _Sodium chloride_

6. Analysis: 68% silver, 22% chlorine, 10% oxygen

Ag: 68% × 100g = 68g / 108g/m = 0.63 m
Cl: 22% × 100g = 22g / 35g/m = 0.63 m
O: 10% × 100g = 10g / 16g/m = 0.63 m

$Ag_{0.63} Cl_{0.63} O_{0.63}$
$Ag_1 Cl_1 O_1$
$Ag_1^{+1} (Cl_1 O_1)^{-1}$

Empirical formula: _____Ag(ClO)_____ Name: _Silver hypochlorite_

7. Analysis: 55% oxygen, 27% phosphorus, 18% lithium

O: 55% × 100g = 55g / 16g/m = 3.4 m
P: 27% × 100g = 27g / 31g/m = 0.87 m
Li: 18% × 100g = 18g / 7g/m = 2.6 m

$O_{\frac{3.4}{0.87}} P_{\frac{0.87}{0.87}} Li_{\frac{2.6}{0.87}}$
$O_4 P_1 Li_3$
$Li_3^{+1} (PO_4)_1^{-3}$

Empirical formula: _Li₃(PO₄)_ Name: _Lithium phosphate_

8. Analysis: 71% bromine, 29% copper

Br: 71% × 100g = 71g / 80g/m = 0.89 m
Cu: 29% × 100g = 29g / 64g/m = 0.45 m

$Br_{\frac{0.89}{0.45}} Cu_{\frac{0.45}{0.45}}$
$Br_2 Cu_1 \rightarrow Cu_1^{+2}$
cations 1st!

Empirical formula: _____CuBr₂_____ Name: _Copper (II) Bromide_

9. Analysis: 40% oxygen, 45% chlorine, 15% magnesium

O: 40% × 100g = 40g / 16g/m = 2.5 m
Cl: 45% × 100g = 45g / 35g = 1.3 m
Mg: 15% × 100g = 15g / 24g = 0.63 m

$Mg_{\frac{0.63}{0.62}} Cl_{\frac{1.3}{0.62}} O_{\frac{2.5}{0.62}}$
$Mg_1 Cl_2 O_4 =$
$Mg(ClO_2)_2$

Empirical formula: _Mg(ClO₂)₂_ Name: _Magnesium chlorite_

Friendly Chemistry

Name_____Date_____
Friendly Chemistry

Lesson 19
Finding Empirical Formulas –2

Below are several analyses of unknown chemical compounds. Find the empirical formula for each compound. Then write the name of that compound in the appropriate space.

1. Analysis: 39% potassium 14% nitrogen 48% oxygen

   K : 39% → 39g / 39g/m = 1m
   N : 14% → 14g / 14g/m = 1m $K_1N_1O_3$
   O : 48% → 48g / 16g/m = 3m $K_1^{+1}(NO_3)_1^{-}$

   Empirical formula: ___$K(NO_3)$___ Name: ___Potassium nitrate___

2. Analysis: 32% sodium 23% sulfur 45% oxygen

   Na : 32% → 32g / 23g/m = 1.4m
   S : 23% → 23g / 32g/m = 0.7m $Na_{\frac{1.4}{0.7}} S_{\frac{0.7}{0.7}} O_{\frac{2.8}{0.7}}$
   O : 45% → 45g / 16g/m = 2.8m $Na_2^{+1}(S_1O_4)_1^{-2}$

   Empirical formula: ___$Na_2(SO_4)$___ Name: ___Sodium sulfate___

3. Analysis: 27% sulfur 33% calcium 40% oxygen

   S : 27% → 27g / 32g/m = 0.8m
   Ca : 33% → 33g / 40g/m = 0.8m $Ca_{\frac{0.8}{0.8}} S_{\frac{0.8}{0.8}} O_{\frac{2.5}{0.8}}$
   O : 40% → 40g / 16g/m = 2.5m $Ca_1^{+2}(S_1O_3)_1^{-2}$

   Empirical formula: ___$Ca(SO_3)$___ Name: ___Calcium sulfite___

4. Analysis: 48% oxygen 35% chlorine 17% chromium

   O : 48% → 48g / 16g/m = 3m
   Cl : 35% → 35g / 35g/m = 1m $Cr_{\frac{.33}{.33}} Cl_{\frac{1}{.33}} O_{\frac{3}{.33}}$
   Cr : 17% → 17g / 52g/m = 0.33m
                                      $Cr_1(Cl_3O_9)$
   Empirical formula: ___$Cr(ClO_3)_3$___ Name: ___Chromium chlorate___

   $Cr_1(Cl_1O_3)_3$

Friendly Chemistry

5. Analysis: 59% oxygen 29% sulfur 13% lithium

O: 59% → 59g / 16g/m = 3.7m
S: 29% → 29g / 32g/m = 0.9m
Li: 13% → 13g / 7g/m = 1.8m

$Li_{1.8} S_{0.9} O_{3.7}$
$\frac{}{0.9}\frac{}{0.9}\frac{}{0.9}$

$Li_2^{+1} (SO_4)_1^{-2}$

Empirical formula: ___$Li_2(SO_4)$___ Name: ___Lithium sulfate___

6. Analysis: 94% sulfur 6% hydrogen

S: 94% → 94g / 32g/m = 2.9m
H: 6% → 6g / 1g/m = 6m

$H_6 S_{2.9}$
$\frac{}{2.9}\frac{}{2.9}$

$H_2^{+1} S_1^{-2}$

Empirical formula: ___H_2S___ Name: ___Hydrogen sulfide___

7. Analysis: 24% nitrogen 21% carbon 55% zinc

N: 24% → 24g / 14g/m = 1.7m
C: 21% → 21g / 12g/m = 1.7m
Zn: 55% → 55g / 65g/m = 0.8m

$Zn_{0.8} C_{1.7} N_{1.7}$
$\frac{}{0.8}\frac{}{0.8}\frac{}{0.8}$

$Zn_1 C_2 N_2$

$Zn_1^{+2} (CN)_2^{-1}$

Empirical formula: ___$Zn(CN)_2$___ Name: ___Zinc cyanide___

8. Analysis: 32% nickel 15% nitrogen 52% oxygen

Ni: 32% → 32g / 52g/m = 0.6m
N: 15% → 15g / 14g/m = 1.1m
O: 52% → 52g / 16g/m = 3.25m

$Ni_{0.6} N_{1.1} O_{3.25}$
$\frac{}{.6}\frac{}{.6}\frac{}{.6}$

$Ni_1 N_2 O_6$

$Ni_1 (NO_3)_2$

Empirical formula: ___$Ni(NO_3)_2$___ Name: ___Nickel nitrate___

9. Analysis: 3% hydrogen 50% chromium 47% oxygen

H: 3% → 3g / 1g/m = 3m
Cr: 50% → 50g / 52g/m = 0.9m
O: 47% → 47g / 16 = 0.9m

$Cr_{.9} O_{.9} H_3$

$Cr_1 (OH)_3$

Empirical formula: ___$Cr(OH)_3$___ Name: ___Chromium hydroxide___

Friendly Chemistry

Name_____ Date_____
Friendly Chemistry

Lesson 19 Test
Finding Empirical Formulas

Below you will see five different analyses for five compounds. Determine the identity of each compound and then write the compound name.

---

1. 64% chlorine, 36% calcium

    Cl: 64% → 64g / 35.5 g/m = 1.8 m $Ca_{0.9}Cl_{1.8}$
    Ca: 36% → 36g / 40 g = 0.9 m
                                            Ca_1Cl_2

    Compound formula: __CaCl$_2$__ Compound Name: ____Calcium chloride____

---

2. 42% nitrogen, 36% carbon, 21% lithium

    N: 42g / 14 g/m = 3 m $Li_3C_3N_3$
    C: 36g / 12 = 3 m
    Li: 21g / 7 = 3 m $Li_1(CN)$

    Compound formula: __Li(CN)_____ Compound Name: _Lithium cyanide_____

---

3. 73% silver, 11% sulfur, 16% oxygen

    Ag: 73g / 108 g/m = 0.68 m $Ag_{0.68/.34}\ S_{0.34/.34}\ O_{1/.34}$
    S: 11g / 32 g/m = 0.34 m
    O: 16g / 16 g/m = 1.0 m $Ag_2S_1O_3$ $Ag_2^{+1}(SO_3)_1^{-2}$

    Compound formula: __Ag$_2$(SO$_3$)__ Compound Name: _Silver sulfite____

---

4. 15% nitrogen, 34% zinc, 51% oxygen

    Zn: 34g / 65 g/m = 0.5 m $Zn_1N_2O_6$
    N: 15g / 14 g/m = 1.1 m
                                      $Zn_1^{+2}(NO_3)_2^{-1}$
    O: 51g / 16 g/m = 3.1

    Compound formula: _Zn(NO$_3$)$_2$__ Compound Name:__Zinc nitrate_

---

5. 19% magnesium, 56% chlorine, 25% oxygen

    Mg: 19g / 24 g/m = 0.8 m $Mg_{0.8}Cl_{1.6}O_{1.6}$
    Cl: 56g / 35 g/m = 1.6 m
    O: 25g / 16 g/m = 1.6 m $Mg_1Cl_2O_2$
                                      $Mg(ClO)_2$

    Compound formula: __Mg(ClO)$_2$__ Compound Name: __Magnesium hypochlorite_

Name_____ Date_____

Friendly Chemistry

Lesson 20
Writing Chemical Reactions

Below you will see several chemical reactions. Re-write these word reactions into chemical formula reactions. The first problem has been completed for you!

1. Hydrogen oxide decomposes into hydrogen gas and oxygen gas.

   $H_2O \longrightarrow H_2 + O_2$

2. Calcium and hydrogen oxide react to yield calcium hydroxide and hydrogen gas.

   $Ca + H_2O \rightarrow Ca(OH)_2 + H_2$

3. Sodium hydroxide and hydrogen chloride react to yield sodium chloride and water.

   $Na(OH) + HCl \rightarrow NaCl + H_2O$

4. Ammonium nitrite decomposes to yield water and nitrogen gas.

   $(NH_4)(NO_2) \rightarrow H_2O + N_2$

5. Hydrogen cyanide and sodium sulfate are the products when hydrogen sulfate and sodium cyanide are combined.

   $H_2(SO_4) + Na(CN) \rightarrow H(CN) + Na_2(SO_4)$

6. Zinc oxide and hydrogen chloride react to yield water and zinc chloride.

   $ZnO + HCl \rightarrow H_2O + ZnCl_2$

7. Elemental carbon © and aluminum oxide react to produce aluminum and carbon dioxide (CO_2).

   $C + Al_2O_3 \rightarrow Al + CO_2$

8. Barium carbonate is the result of the reaction between barium oxide and carbon dioxide.

   $BaO + CO_2 \rightarrow Ba(CO_3)$

9. Potassium chloride and fluorine gas react to yield potassium fluoride and chlorine gas.

   $KCl + F_2 \rightarrow KF + Cl_2$

9. Zinc metal and sulfur react to yield zinc sulfide.

$$Zn + S \rightarrow ZnS$$

11. When calcium is mixed with water, calcium hydroxide and hydrogen gas are produced.

$$Ca + H_2O \rightarrow Ca(OH)_2 + H_2$$

12. Barium carbonate is the product of the reaction between barium oxide and carbon dioxide.

$$BaO + CO_2 \rightarrow Ba(CO_3)$$

13. Hydrogen sulfate and sodium hydroxide react to yield sodium sulfate and water.

$$H_2(SO_4) + Na(OH) \rightarrow Na_2(SO_4) + H_2O$$

14. Water and nitrogen gas react to yield ammonium nitrite.

$$H_2O + N_2 \rightarrow (NH_4)(NO_2)$$

15. Iron and copper (II) sulfate react to yield iron (II) sulfate and copper.

$$Fe + Cu(SO_4) \rightarrow Fe(SO_4) + Cu$$

16. Ammonium chloride and calcium hydroxide react to produce calcium chloride, ammonia (NH_3), and water.

$$(NH_4)Cl + Ca(OH)_2 \rightarrow CaCl_2 + NH_3 + H_2O$$

17. Hydrogen chloride and lead (II) sulfide are the products of the reaction between hydrogen sulfide and lead (II) chloride are combined.

$$H_2S + PbCl_2 \rightarrow HCl + PbS$$

18. Potassium chlorate will decompose quickly into potassium chloride and oxygen gas.

$$K(ClO_3) \rightarrow KCl + O_2$$

Friendly Chemistry

NAME_____ DATE_____
FRIENDLY CHEMISTRY

Lesson 20 Test
Writing Chemical Reactions

Below are 10 chemical reactions written using words. Rewrite them into reactions using chemical formulas and symbols.

1.	sodium hydroxide and hydrogen sulfate react to yield sodium sulfate and water
	$Na(OH) + H_2(SO_4) \rightarrow Na_2(SO_4) + H_2O$
2.	hydrochloric acid (hydrogen chloride) is the product of the reaction of hydrogen gas and chlorine gas
	$H_2 + Cl_2 \rightarrow HCl$
3.	sodium reacts with oxygen to produce sodium oxide
	$Na + O_2 \rightarrow Na_2O$
4.	calcium carbonate and hydrogen sulfate react to yield calcium sulfate, water and carbon dioxide
	$Ca(CO_3) + H_2(SO_4) \rightarrow Ca(SO_4) + H_2O + CO_2$
5.	hydrogen phosphate and sodium hydroxide react to produce sodium phosphate and hydrogen hydroxide
	$H_3(PO_4) + Na(OH) \rightarrow Na_3(PO_4) + H(OH)$
6.	potassium chloride and oxygen gas are the products of the decomposition of potassium perchlorate
	$K(ClO_4) \rightarrow KCl + O_2$
7.	zinc and lead (II) nitrate react to yield zinc nitrate and lead
	$Zn + Pb(NO_3)_2 \rightarrow Zn(NO_3)_2 + Pb$
8.	hydrogen peroxide readily decomposes to produce water and oxygen gas
	$H_2(O_2) \rightarrow H_2O + O_2$
9.	hydrogen iodide decomposes to yield hydrogen gas and iodine (diatomic, too!)
	$HI \rightarrow H_2 + I_2$
10.	calcium hydroxide and hydrogen cyanide are the products when calcium cyanide is dumped into water
	$Ca(CN)_2 + H_2O \rightarrow Ca(OH)_2 + H(CN)$

NAME_____ DATE_____
FRIENDLY CHEMISTRY

Lesson 21
Balancing Chemical Equations –1

Write and balance each chemical equation below. Ask if you need help!

1. hydrogen gas and chlorine gas react to yield hydrogen chloride

$$H_2 + Cl_2 \rightarrow 2HCl$$

2. sodium and oxygen gas react to yield sodium oxide

$$4Na + O_2 \rightarrow 2Na_2O$$

3. calcium carbonate and hydrogen sulfate react to yield calcium sulfate, water and carbon dioxide (CO_2).

$$Ca(CO_3) + H_2(SO_4) \rightarrow Ca(SO_4) + H_2O + CO_2$$

4. hydrogen phosphate and sodium hydroxide react to produce sodium phosphate and water (hint: keep the phosphate as (PO_4) - do not separate!)

$$H_3(PO_4) + 3Na(OH) \rightarrow Na_3(PO_4) + 3H(OH)$$

5. silver nitrate and nickel react to produce nickel nitrate and silver

$$2Ag(NO_3) + Ni \rightarrow Ni(NO_3)_2 + 2Ag$$

6. aluminum sulfate and calcium hydroxide react to yield aluminum hydroxide and calcium sulfate

$$Al_2(SO_4)_3 + 3Ca(OH)_2 \rightarrow 2Al(OH)_3 + 3Ca(SO_4)$$

7. hydrogen iodide decomposes to produce hydrogen gas and iodine (which is I_2).

$$2HI \rightarrow H_2 + I_2$$

8. hydrogen peroxide decomposes to produce water and oxygen gas

$$2H_2(O_2) \rightarrow 2H_2O + O_2$$

9. zinc mixed with lead (II) nitrate yields zinc nitrate and lead

$$Zn + Pb(NO_3)_2 \rightarrow Zn(NO_3)_2 + Pb$$

NAME_____ DATE_____
FRIENDLY CHEMISTRY

Lesson 21 Practice Page –2
Balancing Chemical Equations

Write and balance each chemical equation below. Ask if you need help!

1. potassium fluoride and chlorine gas react to yield potassium chloride and fluorine gas

   $$2KF + Cl_2 \rightarrow 2KCl + F_2$$

2. strontium reacts with oxygen gas to yield strontium oxide

   $$2Sr + O_2 \rightarrow 2SrO$$

3. barium chloride and potassium bromide react to yield potassium chloride, barium and bromine gas

   $$BaCl_2 + 2KBr \rightarrow 2KCl + Ba + Br_2$$

4. water and zinc chloride are the products when zinc oxide and hydrochloric acid (HCl) are mixed.

   $$ZnO + 2HCl \rightarrow H_2O + ZnCl_2$$

5. carbon and aluminum oxide react to yield aluminum and carbon dioxide

$$3C + 2Al_2O_3 \rightarrow 4Al + 3CO_2$$

6. barium oxide and carbon dioxide react to yield barium carbonate

$$BaO + CO_2 \rightarrow Ba(CO_3)$$

7. magnesium carbonate decomposes to produce magnesium oxide and carbon dioxide

$$Mg(CO_3) \rightarrow MgO + CO_2$$

8. ammonium nitrate decomposes to yield nitrogen oxide (N_2O) and water

$$(NH_4)(NO_3) \rightarrow N_2O + 2H_2O$$

9. water decomposes to produce hydrogen gas and oxygen gas.

$$2H_2O \rightarrow 2H_2 + O_2$$

Name _____ Date _____

Friendly Chemistry

Lesson 21 Test
Balancing Chemical Equations

Write and the balance each chemical equation below.

---

1. sodium hydroxide and hydrogen sulfate react to yield sodium sulfate and water

    $2NaOH + H_2(SO_4) \rightarrow Na_2(SO_4) + 2H(OH)$ (or $2H_2O$)

---

2. zinc and lead (II) nitrate react to yield zinc nitrate and lead

    $Zn + Pb(NO_3)_2 \rightarrow Zn(NO_3)_2 + Pb$

---

3. lithium and oxygen gas react to yield lithium oxide

    $4Li + O_2 \rightarrow 2Li_2O$

---

4. aluminum sulfate and calcium hydroxide react to yield aluminum hydroxide and calcium sulfate

    $Al_2(SO_4)_3 + 3Ca(OH)_2 \rightarrow 2Al(OH)_3 + 3Ca(SO_4)$

---

5. calcium cyanide and hydrogen oxide react to yield calcium hydroxide and hydrogen cyanide

    $Ca(CN)_2 + 2H_2O \rightarrow Ca(OH)_2 + 2H(CN)$

Friendly Chemistry

Name_____ Date_____
Friendly Chemistry

Lesson 22: Stoichiometry Practice
Predicting Moles Produced from a Given Amount of Ingredient

1. When hydrogen sulfate and sodium cyanide are mixed, hydrogen cyanide and sodium sulfate are produced. If you begin with 5 moles of sodium cyanide, how many moles of sodium sulfate might you produce from the reaction?

$$H_2(SO_4) + \underline{2Na(CN)} \longrightarrow 2H(CN) + \underline{Na_2(SO_4)}$$
2:1 ratio
5m Na(CN) will yield **2.5 m Na$_2$(SO$_4$)**

2. Zinc oxide and hydrochloric acid react to produce zinc chloride and water. If you begin with 24 moles of zinc oxide, how many moles of zinc chloride will you produce from this reaction?

$$\underline{ZnO} + 2HCl \longrightarrow \underline{ZnCl_2} + H_2O$$
1:1 ratio
24 moles of ZnO will yield **24 moles of ZnCl$_2$**

3. Carbon and aluminum oxide react to produce aluminum and carbon dioxide (CO$_2$). If you have 13 moles of carbon, how many moles of aluminum might you expect to generate from this reaction? Carbon in this reaction will just be C with no subscript or charge.

$$\underline{3C} + 2Al_2O_3 \longrightarrow \underline{4Al} + 3CO_2$$
3:4 ratio
This is a tricky ratio to work with, so let's divide both sides of the ratio by 3. This will give us a ratio of 1:1.33.
13 moles of C will yield 13(1.33)m Al or **17.29 moles Al**

4. When hydrogen gas and iodine gas are mixed, hydrogen iodide is produced. If you began with 0.5 moles of hydrogen gas, how many moles of hydrogen iodide will you potentially produce from this reaction?

$$\underline{H_2} + I_2 \longrightarrow \underline{2HI}$$
1:2 ratio
0.5 moles of hydrogen gas will yield **1 m HI**

5. Barium carbonate is the product of the reaction between barium oxide and carbon dioxide. If you begin with 28 moles of barium oxide, how many moles of barium carbonate could you produce from this reaction?

$$\underline{BaO} + CO_2 \longrightarrow \underline{Ba(CO_3)}$$
Already balanced!
1:1 ratio
28 moles of BaO will yield **28 moles of Ba(CO$_3$)**

6. Magnesium and hydrogen chloride react to produce magnesium chloride and hydrogen gas. Suppose your boss requested you to prepare 65 moles of magnesium chloride from this reaction. When you looked on your shelf you saw that you had 120 moles of hydrogen chloride. Would this be enough to meet your boss' request? Prove your answer with calculations.

$$Mg + \underline{2HCl} \longrightarrow \underline{MgCl_2} + H_2$$
2:1 ratio
120 m of HCl will yield **60 moles of MgCl$_2$**
Your boss needed 65 moles. You won't have enough.

Name_____ Date_____

Friendly Chemistry

Lesson 22: Stoichiometry Practice –2
Predicting Moles Produced from a Given Amount of Ingredient

1. Magnesium chlorate will decompose to produce oxygen gas and magnesium chloride. If you began with 75 moles of magnesium chlorate, how many moles of magnesium chloride can you make from this reaction?

$$Mg(ClO_3)_2 \longrightarrow 3O_2 + MgCl_2$$
1:1 ratio
*75 moles of $Mg(ClO_3)_2$ will yield **75 moles of $MgCl_2$***

2. Iron (III) nitrate and lithium hydroxide react in a double replacement reaction to produce iron (III) hydroxide and lithium nitrate. If Gina began with 34 moles of lithium hydroxide, how many moles of lithium nitrate will she produce from this reaction?

$$Fe(NO_3)_3 + 3Li(OH) \longrightarrow Fe(OH)_3 + 3Li(NO_3)$$
3:3 ratio which reduces to a 1:1 ratio
*34 moles of $Li(OH)$ will yield **34 moles of $Li(NO_3)$***

3. James knew that zinc and sulfur would react to produce zinc sulfide. James had 38 moles of zinc. How many moles of the product could he make in his reaction?

$$Zn + S \longrightarrow ZnS$$
Already balanced!
1:1 ratio
*38 moles of Zn will yield **38 moles of ZnS***

4. Shelly took 5 moles of calcium and placed it into a beaker of bromine gas. Calcium bromide resulted from the reaction that consequently took place. How much calcium bromide did she make from her 5 moles of calcium?

$$Ca + Br_2 \longrightarrow CaBr_2$$
Already balanced!
1:1 ratio
*5 moles of Ca will yield **5 moles of $CaBr_2$***

5. Water will decompose into hydrogen gas and oxygen gas under appropriate conditions. If you begin with 7.8 moles of water, how many moles of hydrogen gas could you produce from this reaction?

$$\underline{2H_2O} \longrightarrow \underline{2H_2} + O_2$$
2:2 ratio which reduces to 1:1
*7.8 moles of water will yield **7.8 moles of H_2***

6. Lead (II) nitrate and zinc readily react to produce zinc nitrate and lead. How many moles lead could you produce from 40 moles of zinc?

$$Pb(NO_3)_2 + \underline{Zn} \longrightarrow Zn(NO_3)_2 + \underline{Pb}$$
Already balanced!
1:1 ratio
*40 moles of Zn will yield **40 moles of Pb***

7. Lye (sodium hydroxide) and hydrogen sulfate react to produce sodium sulfate and water. If you begin with 4.5 moles of lye, how many moles of water could you produce from this reaction?

$$\underline{2Na(OH)} + H_2(SO_4) \longrightarrow Na_2(SO_4) + \underline{2H(OH)}$$
Note in this reaction we chose to write water as H(OH) as opposed to H_2O. We did this because we noted there was an (OH) on the reactant side of reaction. Instead of separating the H's and O's, we can leave them together as (OH)'s on both sides. This makes the balancing process easier.
Ratio is 2:2 which reduces to 1:1.
*4.5 moles of Na(OH) will yield **4.5 moles of water.***

NAME_____ DATE_____
FRIENDLY CHEMISTRY

Lesson 22 Test
Introduction to Stoichiometry

Read each problem below. Predict the requested amount of product from the information given. Take your time and check your work when done..

1. When sodium is placed into oxygen gas, sodium oxide is produced. If you begin with 5 moles of sodium how many moles of sodium oxide can you expect to make from this reaction?

    Our reaction is: $\underline{4Na} + O_2 \longrightarrow \underline{2Na_2O_1}$; *Mole ratio = 4:2 = 2:1*
    If we begin with 5 moles of sodium, based upon the mole ratio, we should produce
    2.5 moles of sodium oxide.

2. Hydrogen nitrate and sodium hydroxide react to produce sodium nitrate and hydrogen hydroxide (water). If you begin with 10 moles of sodium hydroxide, how many moles of sodium nitrate can you expect to generate from this reaction?

    Our reaction is $H(NO_3) + \underline{Na(OH)} \longrightarrow \underline{Na(NO_3)} + H(OH)$; *mole ratio is 1:1*
    If you begin with 10 moles of sodium hydroxide, based upon the mole ratio, you should produce **10 moles of sodium nitrate**.

3. Ammonium nitrate will decompose to produce nitrogen oxide (N_2O) and water. If you begin with 3.5 moles of ammonium nitrate, how many moles of water can you expect to make from this reaction?

    Our reaction is: $\underline{(NH_4)(NO_3)} \longrightarrow N_2O + \underline{2H_2O}$; *Mole ratio is 1:2*
    If you begin with 3.5 moles of ammonium nitrate, based upon the mole ratio, you should produce **7 moles of water**.

4. Aluminum sulfate and calcium hydroxide react to yield aluminum hydroxide and calcium sulfate. If you begin with 0.5 moles of calcium hydroxide, how many moles of aluminum hydroxide can you produce from this reaction?

Our reaction is: $Al_2(SO_4)_3 + 3\underline{Ca(OH)_2} \longrightarrow 2\underline{Al(OH)_3} + 3Ca(SO_4)$; *mole ratio is 3:2 = 1: 0.66 ratio*
If we begin the reaction with 0.5 moles of calcium hydroxide, we should be able to produce (0.5 x 0.66) = **0.33 m $Al(OH)_3$**

5. Calcium cyanide and water react to yield calcium hydroxide and hydrogen cyanide. If you begin with 13 moles of water, how many moles of calcium hydroxide can you expect to produce from this reaction?

$Ca(CN)_2 + \underline{2H(OH)} \longrightarrow \underline{Ca(OH)_2} + 2H(CN)$; *mole ratio is 2:1.*
If we begin with 13 moles of water, we should produce **6.5 moles of hydrogen cyanide**.

6. Magnesium oxide and carbon dioxide are the products from the decomposition of magnesium carbonate. If you begin with 8 moles of magnesium carbonate, how many moles of magnesium oxide can you expect to make from this reaction?

Our reaction is: $\underline{Mg(CO_3)} \longrightarrow MgO + CO_2$ *Mole ratio is 1:1*
If we begin with 8 moles of magnesium carbonate, we could expect to produce
8 moles of magnesium oxide.

Name_____ Date_____

Friendly Chemistry

Lesson 23: Stoichiometry Practice –1
Predicting Grams Produced from a Given Amount of Ingredient

1. When hydrogen sulfate and sodium cyanide are mixed, hydrogen cyanide and sodium sulfate are the produced. If you begin with 25 moles of sodium cyanide, how many **grams** of sodium sulfate might you produce from the reaction?

$$H_2(SO_4) + \underline{2Na(CN)} \longrightarrow 2H(CN) + \underline{Na_2(SO_4)}$$
2:1 ratio
25 moles of Na(CN) will yield 12.5 moles of $Na_2(SO_4)$
1 mole $Na_2(SO_4)$ has a formula weight of 142 grams.
12.5 moles of $Na_2(SO_4)$ will therefore have a mass of **1775 grams**.
(12.5 m x 142 g/m = 1775 g)

2. Zinc oxide and hydrochloric acid react to produce zinc chloride and water. If you begin with 14 moles of zinc oxide, how many **grams** of zinc chloride will you produce from this reaction?

$$\underline{ZnO} + 2HCl \longrightarrow \underline{ZnCl_2} + H_2O$$
1:1 ratio
14 moles of ZnO will yield 14 moles of $ZnCl_2$
1 mole of $ZnCl_2$ has a formula weight of 135 g.
14 moles of $ZnCl_2$ will have a mass of **1890 g.**
(14 m x 135 g/m = 1890 g)

3. Carbon and aluminum oxide react to produce aluminum and carbon dioxide (CO_2). If you have 1.4 moles of carbon, how many **grams** of aluminum might you expect to generate from this reaction?

$$\underline{3C} + 2Al_2O_3 \longrightarrow \underline{4Al} + 3CO_2$$
3:4 ratio which can be reduced to 1:1.33 (divide both sides by 3).
1.4 m C will yield 1.86 m Al.
1 m of Al has a formula weight (atomic mass) of 27 grams.
1.86 m of Al will have a mass of **50.22 grams.**
(1.86 x 27g/m = 50.22 grams).

4. When hydrogen gas and iodine gas are mixed, hydrogen iodide is produced. If you began with 74 moles of hydrogen gas, how many **grams** of hydrogen iodide will you potentially produce from this reaction?

$$H_2 + I_2 \longrightarrow 2HI$$
1:2 ratio
74 m of H_2 will yield 148 m of HI
1 m HI has a formula weight of 128 grams.
148 moles of HI will have a mass of **18,944 grams**.
(148m x 128g/m = 18,944 grams)

5. Barium carbonate is the product of the reaction between barium oxide and carbon dioxide. If you begin 0.4 moles of barium oxide, how many **grams** of barium carbonate could you produce from this reaction?

$$BaO + CO_2 \longrightarrow Ba(CO_3)$$
1:1 ratio
0.4 moles of BaO will yield 0.4 moles of $Ba(CO_3)$
1 mole of $Ba(CO_3)$ has a formula weight of 197 grams.
0.4 m $Ba(CO_3)$ will have a mass of **78.8 grams**.
(0.4 m x 197g/m = 78.8 grams).

6. Magnesium and hydrogen chloride react to produce magnesium chloride and hydrogen gas. If you begin with 4.6 moles of magnesium, how many **grams** of magnesium chloride can you produce from this reaction?

$$Mg + 2HCl \longrightarrow MgCl_2 + H_2$$
1:1 ratio
4.6 moles of Mg will result in 4.6 moles of $MgCl_2$
1 mole $MgCl_2$ has a formula weight of 94 grams.
4.6 moles of $MgCl_2$ will have a mass of **432.4 grams**.
(4.6 x 94 g/mole = 432.4 grams)

Name_____ Date_____
Friendly Chemistry

Lesson 23: Stoichiometry Practice –2
Predicting Grams Produced from a Given Amount of Ingredient

1. Magnesium chlorate will decompose to produce oxygen gas and magnesium chloride. If you began with 7.05 moles of magnesium chlorate, how many **grams** of magnesium chloride can you make from this reaction?

$$\underline{Mg(ClO_3)_2} \longrightarrow 3O_2 + \underline{MgCl_2}$$
1:1 ratio
7.05 moles of $Mg(ClO_3)_2$ will yield 7.05 moles of $MgCl_2$
1 mole of $MgCl_2$ has a formula weight of 94 grams.
7.05 moles of MgCl2 will have a mass of **662.7 grams**.

2. Iron (III) nitrate and lithium hydroxide react in a double replacement reaction to produce iron (III) hydroxide and lithium nitrate. If Morris began with 13 moles of lithium hydroxide, how many **grams** of lithium nitrate will she produce from this reaction?

$$Fe(NO_3)_3 + \underline{3Li(OH)} \longrightarrow Fe(OH)_3 + \underline{3Li(NO_3)}$$
3:3 ratio which reduces to a 1:1 ratio
13 moles of Li(OH) will yield 13 moles of $Li(NO_3)$
1 mole of $Li(NO_3)$ weighs 69 grams.
13 moles of $Li(NO_3)$ will then weigh **897 grams**.

3. Jon knew that zinc and sulfur would react to produce zinc sulfide. Jon had 38 moles of zinc. How many **grams** of the product could he make in his reaction?

$$\underline{Zn} + S \longrightarrow \underline{ZnS}$$
1:1 ratio
38 moles of Zn will yield 38 moles of ZnS
1 mole of ZnS weighs 97 grams.
38 moles of ZnS will then weigh **3686 grams.**

4. Tori took 0.97 moles of calcium and placed it into a beaker of bromine gas. Calcium bromide resulted from the reaction that consequently took place. How many **grams** of calcium bromide did she make from her 0.97 moles of calcium?

$$\underline{Ca} + Br_2 \longrightarrow \underline{CaBr_2}$$
1:1 ratio
0.97 moles of Ca will yield 0.97 moles of $CaBr_2$
1 mole of $CaBr_2$ weighs 200 grams.
0.97 moles of CaBr2 will have a mass of **194 grams**.

5. Water will decompose into hydrogen gas and oxygen gas when an electric current is applied to it. If you begin with 24 moles of water, how many **moles** of hydrogen gas could you produce from this reaction?

$$\underline{2H_2O} \longrightarrow \underline{2H_2} + O_2$$
1:1 ratio
24 moles of water will yield **24 moles of H_2**

6. Lead (II) nitrate and zinc readily react to produce zinc nitrate and lead. How many **grams** of lead could you produce from 9 moles of zinc?

$$Pb(NO_3)_2 + \underline{Zn} \longrightarrow Zn(NO_3)_2 + \underline{Pb}$$
1:1 ratio
9 moles of Zn will yield 9 moles of Pb
1 mole of Pb weighs 207 grams, therefore 9 moles will weigh 9 x 207 = **1863 g**

7. Lye (sodium hydroxide) and hydrogen sulfate react to produce sodium sulfate and water. If you begin with 4.5 moles of lye, how many **grams** of water could you produce from this reaction?

$$\underline{2Na(OH)} + H_2(SO_4) \longrightarrow Na_2(SO_4) + \underline{2H(OH)}$$
1:1 ratio
4.5 moles sodium hydroxide will yield 4.5 moles of water
1 mole of water weighs 18 grams, therefore 4.5 moles will weigh 4.5 x 18 = **81 g**

8. When lithium metal is exposed to oxygen gas, a rapid reaction takes place resulting with the production of lithium oxide. If you begin with 3.2 moles of lithium, how many **grams** of lithium oxide can you expect to produce from the reaction?

$$\underline{4Li} + O_2 \longrightarrow \underline{2Li_2O}$$
2:1 ratio
3.2 moles of lithium will yield 1.6 moles of lithium oxide.
One mole of lithium oxide weighs 30 grams.
1.6 moles of lithium oxide will weigh 1.6 x 30 grams = **48 grams**.

NAME_____   DATE_____
FRIENDLY CHEMISTRY

Lesson 23 Test
Predicting Grams of Product

Read each problem below. Predict the requested amount of product from the information given. Take your time and check your work when done..

1. Iron (III) nitrate and lithium hydroxide react to produce iron (III) hydroxide and lithium nitrate. If you began with 10 moles of lithium hydroxide, how many grams of lithium nitrate will she produce from this reaction?

Here is our reaction: $Fe(NO_3)_3$ + 3Li(OH) —> $Fe(OH)_3$ + 3Li(NO_3); Mole ratio is 3:3 or 1:1. We are beginning with 10 moles of Li(OH), so we can go ahead and apply the mole ratio. 10 moles of Li(OH) will produce 10 moles of Li(NO_3).
*We've been asked to find the number of grams of lithium nitrate produced, so we'll need to convert our last result from moles into grams. One mole of Li(NO_3) has a formula weight of 69 grams. 10 moles x 69 grams per mole = **690 grams Li(NO_3)**.*

2. Hydrogen nitrate and sodium hydroxide react to produce sodium nitrate and hydrogen hydroxide (water). If you begin with 22 moles of sodium hydroxide, how many grams of sodium nitrate can you expect to generate from this reaction?

Our reaction is: H(NO_3) + Na(OH) —> Na(NO_3) + H(OH); Mole ratio is 1:1. We are beginning with 22 moles of Na(OH). We can apply the mole ratio. 22 moles of Na(OH) will produce 22 moles of Na(NO_3). One mole of Na(NO_3) has a formula weight of 85 grams.
*22 moles x 85 grams per mole = **1870 grams Na(NO_3)**.*

3. Frankie took 48.5 moles of calcium and placed it into a beaker of bromine gas. Calcium bromide resulted from the reaction that consequently took place. How many grams of calcium bromide did he make from his 48.5 moles of calcium?

Our reaction is: Ca + Br_2 —> $CaBr_2$; Mole ratio is 1:1.
*We are beginning with 48.5 moles of Ca. Applying the mole ratio we can say that 48.5 moles of Ca can produce 48.5 moles of $CaBr_2$. One mole of $CaBr_2$ has a formula weight of 200 grams. 48.5 moles x 200 grams per mole = **9700 grams $CaBr_2$**.*

4. Ammonium nitrate will decompose to produce nitrogen oxide (N_2O) and water. If you begin with 7.3 moles of ammonium nitrate, how many <u>grams</u> of nitrogen oxide can you expect to make from this reaction?

   Here is our reaction: <u>$(NH_4)(NO_3)$</u> —> <u>N_2O</u> + $2H_2O$; Mole ratio is 1:1.
We are beginning with 7.3 moles of $(NH_4)(NO_3)$. By applying the mole ratio, we can say that 7.3 moles of $(NH_4)(NO_3)$ will produce 7.3 moles of N_2O.
   One mole of N_2O has a formula weight of 44 grams.
   7.3 moles x 44 grams per mole = **321.2 grams N_2O.**

5. Aluminum sulfate and calcium hydroxide react to yield aluminum hydroxide and calcium sulfate. If you begin with 0.25 moles of calcium hydroxide, how many <u>grams</u> of calcium sulfate can you produce from this reaction?

   $Al_2(SO_4)_3$ + <u>$3Ca(OH)_2$</u> —> $2Al(OH)_3$ + <u>$3Ca(SO_4)$</u>; Mole ratio is 3:3 = 1:1.
We are beginning with 0.25 moles of $Ca(OH)_2$. By applying the mole ratio we can say that 0.25 moles of $Ca(OH)_2$ will produce 0.25 moles of $Ca(SO_4)$.
   One mole of $Ca(SO_4)$ has a formula weight of 136 grams.
   0.25 moles x 136 grams per mole = **34 grams $Ca(SO_4)$.**

Name_____ Date_____
Friendly Chemistry

Lesson 24: Stoichiometry Practice –1
Predicting Grams Produced from a Given Amount of Grams of Reactant

1. Carbon and aluminum oxide react to produce aluminum and carbon dioxide (CO_2). Suppose that Tony has 48 **grams** of carbon, how many **grams** of aluminum might he expect to generate from this reaction?

$$\underline{3C} + 2Al_2O_3 \longrightarrow \underline{4Al} + 3CO_2$$

3:4 ratio which can be converted to a 1:1.33 ratio
Tony has 48 grams; we'll need to convert that to moles first. One mole of carbon weighs 12 grams, therefore Tony has 4 moles of C (48/12 = 4).
Let's apply the mole ratio: 4 moles of C will yield 4 x 1.33 = 5.32 moles of Al. One mole of Al weighs 27 grams, therefore 5.32 moles will weigh **143.6 grams Al.**

2. Zinc oxide and hydrochloric acid react to produce zinc chloride and water. If you begin with 78 grams of zinc oxide, how many grams of zinc chloride will you produce from this reaction?

$$\underline{ZnO} + 2HCl \longrightarrow \underline{ZnCl_2} + H_2O$$

1:1 ratio. You begin with 78 g of zinc oxide; we'll need to convert that to moles first. One mole of zinc oxide weighs 81 grams. Therefore 78 grams/81 grams per mole = 0.96 moles. Apply the ratio: 0.96 m ZnO will yield 0.96 moles $ZnCl_2$. Now convert this result back to grams. One mole of zinc chloride weighs 135 grams. So, 0.96 moles would weigh **129.6 grams zinc chloride**.

3. When hydrogen sulfate and sodium cyanide are mixed, hydrogen cyanide and sodium sulfate are the produced. Suppose Chuck has 100 grams of hydrogen sulfate. How many grams of hydrogen cyanide might he expect to produce from this reaction?

$$\underline{H_2(SO_4)} + 2Na(CN) \longrightarrow \underline{2H(CN)} + Na_2(SO_4)$$

1:2 ratio
Chuck has 100 grams; let's convert that to moles first. One mole of hydrogen sulfate weighs 98 grams. 100 grams/98 grams per mole = 1.02 moles. Apply the ratio: 1.02 moles hydrogen sulfate will yield 2.04 moles hydrogen cyanide. Now, convert this back to grams. One mole of hydrogen cyanide weighs 27 grams. 2.04 moles x 27 grams per mole = **55.08 grams H(CN).**

4. Mary had 456 grams of barium oxide. She knew that barium carbonate is the product of the reaction between barium oxide and carbon dioxide. If she used all of her barium oxide in the reaction, how many grams of barium carbonate might she expect to produce?

$$\underline{BaO} + CO_2 \longrightarrow \underline{Ba(CO_3)}$$

1:1 ratio; Mary started with 456 grams. Convert this to moles. One mole of BaO weighs 153 grams, so 456 grams/153 grams per mole = 2.98 moles. Apply the mole ratio: 2.98 moles of BaO will yield 2.98 moles of barium carbonate. Convert these moles back to grams: one mole of barium carbonate weighs 197 grams. 2.98 moles x 197 grams per mole = **587.06 grams barium carbonate.**

5. When hydrogen gas and iodine gas are mixed, hydrogen iodide is produced. Sara's boss needed her to prepare some hydrogen iodide for a procedure they were doing later that day. If Sara had 3000 grams of iodine gas on hand, how many grams of hydrogen iodide could she make for her boss?

$$H_2 + I_2 \longrightarrow 2HI$$

1:2 ratio. Sara had 3000 grams of I_2. Convert this to moles. One mole of I_2 weighs 252 grams. 3000 grams / 254 g/mole = 11.8 moles. Apply the mole ratio: 11.8 moles of I_2 will yield 23.6 moles of HI. Now, convert this back to grams. One mole of HI weighs 128 grams. 23.6 moles x 128 g/mole = **3020.8. grams HI**

6. Magnesium and hydrogen chloride react to produce magnesium chloride and hydrogen gas. If you begin with 4.6 **moles** of magnesium, how many grams of magnesium chloride can you produce from this reaction?

$$Mg + 2HCl \longrightarrow MgCl_2 + H_2$$

1:1 ratio. We're starting with moles of magnesium in this problem (as opposed to grams in the rest of the previous problems.) So, we can go ahead and apply the mole ratio: 4.6 moles of magnesium will produce 4.6 moles of magnesium chloride. We are being asked how many grams of magnesium chloride could be produced, so we'll need to convert our current answer to grams. One mole of magnesium chloride weighs 94 grams. Therefore 4.6 moles x 94 grams per mole = **432.4 grams $MgCl_2$.**

Name_____ Date_____

Friendly Chemistry

Lesson 24: Stoichiometry Practice –2
Predicting Grams Produced from a Given Amount of Grams of Reactant

1. Franklin found in his chemistry manual that magnesium chlorate will decompose to produce oxygen gas and magnesium chloride. If he began with 3 kg of magnesium chlorate, how many kilograms of magnesium chloride could he make from this reaction? (one kilogram = 1000g and atomic mass values are always given in grams).

$$\underline{Mg(ClO_3)_2} \longrightarrow 3O_2 + \underline{MgCl_2}$$

1:1 ratio. Franklin has 3000 grams of magnesium chlorate. We'll convert that to moles first. One mole of magnesium chlorate weighs 190 grams. 3000 grams / 190g per mole = 15.8 moles. Apply the mole ratio: 15.8 moles of magnesium chlorate will yield 15.8 moles of magnesium chloride. Convert this back to grams. One mole of magnesium chloride weighs 94 grams. 15.8 moles x 94 grams per mole = **1485 grams**. *The question asks for our answer in kilograms, so we'll divide by 1000 to find that Franklin produced* **1.485 kg** *of magnesium chloride.*

2. Iron (III) nitrate and lithium hydroxide react in a double replacement reaction to produce iron (III) hydroxide and lithium nitrate. If Sheila began with 74 grams of lithium hydroxide, how many grams of lithium nitrate will she produce from this reaction?

$$Fe(NO_3)_3 + \underline{3Li(OH)} \longrightarrow Fe(OH)_3 + \underline{3Li(NO_3)}$$

3:3 ratio which reduces to a 1:1 ratio. Shelia begins with 74 grams of Li(OH). Convert that to moles. One mole of Li(OH) weighs 24 grams. 74/24 grams per mole = 3.08 moles. Apply the mole ratio: 3.08 m of Li(OH) will produce 3.08 moles of lithium nitrate. Convert back to grams now. One mole of lithium nitrate weighs 69 grams. So, 3.08 m x 69 grams = **212.52 grams lithium nitrate**.

3. Jeremy knew that zinc and sulfur would react to produce zinc sulfide. If Jeremy had half a bottle of zinc pellets available for his reaction, how many grams of zinc sulfide could he produce? The bottle originally held 1500 grams of zinc.

$$\underline{Zn} + \underline{S} \longrightarrow \underline{ZnS}$$

1:1 ratio. Jeremy's bottle was half-full, so 1500g/2 = 750 grams. Convert to moles. One mole of zinc weighs 65 grams. 750/65 g per mole = 11.5 moles. Apply the mole ratio. 11.5 moles of zinc will yield 11.5 moles of ZnS. Convert back to grams. One mole of ZnS weighs 97 grams. 11.5 x 97g = **1115.5 grams ZnS**.

4. Billy took 350 grams of calcium and placed it into a beaker of bromine gas. Calcium bromide resulted from the reaction that consequently took place. His instructor needed at least 400 grams of calcium bromide for a class project. Could Billy make enough with this 350 grams? Show proof of your answer with calculations.

$$\underline{Ca} + \underline{Br_2} \longrightarrow \underline{CaBr_2}$$

1:1 ratio. Convert 350g to moles. One m Ca = 40g. 350/40 g per mole = 8.75 m. Apply mole ratio. 8.75 moles will yield 8.75 moles. One mole of CaBr weighs 200 grams; 8.75 m x 200 g per mole = **1750 grams CaBr₂. Yes, Billy would have enough.**

5. Hydrogen gas and oxygen gas are the products of the decomposition of water. If you took 50 mls of water and allowed it all decompose into hydrogen and oxygen gas, how many grams of oxygen gas might you yield from this reaction? (1 ml of water = 1 gram of water).

$$2H_2O \longrightarrow 2H_2 + O_2$$
2:1 ratio

50 mls water =- 50 grams of water. Convert to moles. One mole of water = 18 grams. 50/18 g per mole = 2.78 moles. Apply the mole ratio: 2.77 moles of water will yield 1.39 moles of O_2. Convert this result back to grams. One mole of oxygen gas has a mass of 32 grams. 1.39 moles x 32 g/mole = **44.48 grams oxygen gas**.

6. Lead (II) nitrate and zinc readily react to produce zinc nitrate and lead. How many grams of lead could you produce from 5 grams of lead (II) nitrate?

$$Pb(NO_3)_2 + Zn \longrightarrow Zn(NO_3)_2 + Pb$$
1:1 ratio

5 grams of lead (II) nitrate must be converted to moles of lead (II) nitrate. One mole of $Pb(NO_3)_2$ = 331 grams. 5 grams/331 g/mole = 0.015 moles. Apply the mole ratio: .015 moles of lead (II) nitrate will produce 0.015 moles Pb. Convert back to grams. 0.015 moles x 207g/mole = **3.1 grams Pb.**

7. When lithium metal is exposed to oxygen gas, a rapid reaction takes place resulting with the production of lithium oxide. If you begin with 6700 grams of lithium, how many grams of lithium oxide can you expect to produce from the reaction?

$$4Li + O_2 \longrightarrow 2Li_2O$$
2:1 ratio

We are beginning with 6700 grams of lithium. We need to convert this to moles. One mole of Li = 7 grams, so 6700g / 7 g/mole = 957 moles of Li. Apply the mole ratio: 957 moles of Li will yield 478.5 moles of Li_2O. Convert these moles back into grams. One mole of Li_2O weighs 30 grams. 478.5 moles x 30g/mole = **14,355 grams lithium oxide**.

NAME_____ DATE_____
FRIENDLY CHEMISTRY

Lesson 24 Test
Predicting Grams of Product from Given Grams of Reactant

Read each problem below. Predict the requested amount of product from the information given. Take your time and check over your work when done. Show all work!

1. Nitric acid (hydrogen nitrate) and sodium hydroxide react to yield sodium nitrate and water. If you begin with 45 **grams** of sodium hydroxide, how many **grams** sodium nitrate can you yield from this reaction?

*Here is our reaction: $H(NO_3)$ + $Na(OH)$ —> $Na(NO_3)$ + $H(OH)$; mole ratio 1:1
We are beginning with 45 grams of Na(OH). We'll need to convert this into moles before applying the mole ratio. One mole of Na(OH) has a formula weight of 40 grams. 40 grams = 1.125 moles. Now we can apply the mole ratio: 1.125 moles of Na(OH) will yield 1.125 moles of $Na(NO_3)$. We are asked to predict the number of grams being produced. We'll need a formula weight for our product: $Na(NO_3)$ = 85 grams per mole. Our reaction produced 1.125 moles, therefore, 1.125 x 85 g per mole =*
95.6 grams.

2. When bromine gas is bubbled through calcium, calcium bromide is produced. If you begin with 80 **grams** of calcium, how many **grams** of calcium bromide can you yield from this reaction?

*Here is our reaction: Br_2 + Ca —> $CaBr_2$; Mole ratio: 1:1
We are beginning with 80 grams of Ca. We need to convert this to moles. One mole of Ca = 40 g, therefore, 80 g = 2 moles Ca. Applying the mole ratio, we see that 2 moles of Ca will produce 2 moles of $CaBr_2$. We are asked to find grams of $CaBr_2$. One mole of $CaBr_2$ = 200 grams. 2 moles of $CaBr_2$ = 2 x 200 grams per mole =*
400 grams $CaBr_2$.

3. Zinc oxide and hydrochloric acid react to yield zinc chloride and water. If Hank begins with 400 **grams** of zinc oxide, how many **grams** of zinc chloride can you produce from this reaction?

*Our reaction is: ZnO + $2HCl$ —> $ZnCl_2$ + H_2O; Mole ratio: 1:1
One mole of ZnO = 81 g. 400 g/81 grams per mole = 4.9 moles.
We can now apply the mole ratio: 4.9 moles of ZnO will produce 4.9 moles of $ZnCl_2$.
We need to convert these moles back into grams for the final answer.
One mole of $ZnCl_2$ has a formula weight of 135 grams.
4.9 moles x 135 grams per mole = **661.5 grams***

5. Hydrogen cyanide gas and sodium sulfate are produced from the reaction of hydrogen sulfate and sodium cyanide. If you begin with 30 **grams** of sodium cyanide, how many **grams** of sodium sulfate can you produce from this reaction?

*Our reaction is: $H_2(SO_4)$ + 2Na(CN) —> 2H(CN) + $Na_2(SO_4)$; Mole ratio: 2:1.
One mole of Na(CN) has a formula weight of 49 grams. 30 grams/49 grams per mole = 0.61 moles. We can apply the mole ratio: 0.61 moles of Na(CN) will produce 0.305 moles of $Na_2(SO_4)$. We need to convert this result back to moles. One mole of $Na_2(SO_4)$ has a formula weight of 142 grams.
0.305 moles x 142 grams per mole = **43.3 grams $Na_2(SO_4)$.***

6. Aluminum oxide and carbon will react to yield aluminum and carbon dioxide. If you begin with a full container of aluminum oxide (the label reads 500 **grams**) and expose all of it to carbon, how many **grams** of aluminum might you yield from this reaction?

*Here is our reaction: $2Al_2O_3$ + 3C —> 4Al + $3CO_2$; Mole ratio: 1:2
One mole of Al_2O_3 has a formula weight of 102 grams. 500 grams/102 grams per mole = 4.9 moles aluminum oxide. We can now apply the mole ratio: 4.9 moles of aluminum oxide will yield 9.8 moles of Al. We've been asked to find the number of grams of Al produced by the reaction. One mole of aluminum weighs 27 grams.
9.8 moles x 27 grams per mole = **264.6 grams***

Friendly Chemistry

Name_____   Date_____

Friendly Chemistry

Lesson 25: Stoichiometry Practice –1
How Much Reactant Do I Need?

1. When zinc is dropped into sulfuric acid (hydrogen sulfate), zinc sulfate and hydrogen gas are produced. If you needed to produce 40 moles of zinc sulfate, how many moles of zinc would this require?

   $\underline{Zn} + H_2(SO_4) \longrightarrow \underline{Zn(SO_4)} + H_2$
   Already balanced!
   1:1 ratio
   *Making 40 moles of zinc sulfate would require **40 moles of zinc**.*

2. Iron and copper (II) sulfate react to produce iron (II) sulfate and copper. If you needed to produce 34 moles of copper from this reaction, how many moles of iron would be required?

   $\underline{Fe} + Cu(SO_4) \longrightarrow Fe(SO_4) + \underline{Cu}$
   Already balanced.
   1:1 ratio
   *Making 34 moles of copper would require **34 moles of iron**.*

3. Ammonium chloride and calcium hydroxide react to yield calcium chloride, ammonia (NH_3), and water. If your boss asked you to prepare 45 moles of calcium chloride from this reaction, how many **grams** of ammonium chloride would you need to have ready?

   $\underline{2(NH_4)Cl} + Ca(OH)_2 \longrightarrow \underline{CaCl_2} + 2NH_3 + 2H(OH)$
   2:1 ratio
   *To produce 45 moles of calcium chloride would require 90 moles of ammonium chloride. One mole of ammonium chloride has a formula weight of 53 grams. 90 moles x 53 grams/mole = **4770 grams of ammonium chloride**.*

4. Lead (II) sulfide can be produced from the reaction of hydrogen sulfide and lead (II) chloride. Hydrogen chloride is a byproduct of the reaction. If you needed to prepare 400 moles of lead (II) sulfide, how many grams of EACH reactant will you need? Hint: determine two separate mole ratios.

$$H_2S + PbCl_2 \longrightarrow PbS + 2HCl$$

Looking at the amount of hydrogen sulfide needed, we see that this is a 1:1 ratio. To produce 400 moles of lead (II) sulfide, we'd need 400 moles of hydrogen sulfide. One mole of hydrogen sulfide has a formula weight of 34 grams. Therefore, 400 moles of hydrogen sulfide would have a mass of (34 x 400) **13,600 grams**.

Now, to find the amount of lead (II) chloride needed, again we see this is a 1:1 ratio. To produce 400 moles of lead sulfide, we'd need 400 moles of lead (II) chloride. One mole of lead (II) chloride has a mass of 277 grams. Therefore, 400 moles of lead (II) chloride would have a mass of **110,800 grams**.

5. Ammonia (NH_3) reacts with hydrogen sulfide to produce ammonium sulfide. If you need 2.3 moles of ammonium sulfide, how many grams of ammonia would you need?

$$2NH_3 + H_2S \longrightarrow (NH_4)_2S$$
2:1 ratio

In order to make 2.3 moles of ammonium sulfide, we would need 4.6 moles of ammonia. One mole of ammonia has a formula weight of 17 grams. Therefore, 4.6 moles would have a mass of (4.6 x 17 gram) **78.2 grams ammonia**.

Friendly Chemistry

Name_____ Date_____
Friendly Chemistry

Lesson 25: Stoichiometry Practice –2
How Much Reactant Do I Need?

1. Potassium chloride, when exposed to oxygen gas, produces potassium perchlorate. If you need to produce 13 moles of potassium perchlorate, how many grams of potassium chloride would you need?

$$\underline{KCl} + 2O_2 \longrightarrow \underline{K(ClO_4)}$$
1:1 ratio
Producing 13 moles of potassium perchlorate would require 13 moles of potassium chloride. One mole of KCl has a formula weight of 74 grams. Therefore, 13 moles would weigh (13 x 74 g) **962 grams**.

2. When iron is exposed to oxygen gas, rust (Iron (III) oxide) forms. If you begin with 25 grams of iron, how many grams of iron (III) oxide can you **produce** from this reaction?

$$\underline{4Fe} + 3O_2 \longrightarrow \underline{2Fe_2O_3}$$
4:2 ratio, which reduces to 2:1
25 grams of iron is equivalent to 0.44 moles (25 g / 56 g/m = 0.44 moles). Apply the mole ratio: 0.44 moles of Fe would yield 0.22 moles of iron (III) oxide. Now, we just need to convert this back to grams. One mole of iron (III) oxide has a formula weight of 160 grams. 0.22 moles x 160 g/m = **35.2 grams iron (III) oxide** *(rust).*

3. Ammonium sulfide decomposes to produce ammonia and hydrogen sulfide. If you begin with 3 pounds of ammonium sulfide, how many grams of hydrogen sulfide might you expect to **produce** from this reaction? Note that 1 pound = 454 grams!

$$\underline{(NH_4)_2S} \longrightarrow 2NH_3 + \underline{H_2S}$$
1:1 ratio
3 pounds of ammonium sulfide = 3(454 grams per pound) = 1362 grams ammonium sulfide which is what we are beginning with. Let's convert this to moles. One mole of ammonium sulfide has a formula weight of 68 grams. 1362 grams/68 grams per mole = 20 moles of ammonium sulfide. Apply the mole ratio: 20 moles of ammonium sulfide will produce 20 moles of hydrogen sulfide. Convert this result back to grams. One mole of H_2S has a mass of 34 grams.
20 moles x 34 grams per mole = **680 grams hydrogen sulfide**.

4. If bromine gas is bubbled through potassium iodide, potassium bromide and iodine crystals are produced. Suppose you need to make 100 grams of iodine crystals. How many grams of potassium iodide do you need?

$$Br_2 + \underline{2KI} \longrightarrow 2KBr + \underline{I_2}$$
2:1 ratio

We are asked to make 100 grams of iodine crystals (note iodine crystals are diatomic). We need to convert this desired amount to moles first. One mole of I_2 has a formula weight of 254 grams. 100 grams/254 grams per mole = 0.39 moles.
Apply the mole ratio: to make 0.39 moles of iodine crystals, we'd need 0.78 moles of potassium iodide (KI). Now, let's convert this result back to grams.
One mole of potassium iodide has a formula weight of 166 grams.
0.78 moles x 166 grams/mole = **129.48 grams**

5. When aluminum is combined with sulfuric acid (hydrogen sulfate), aluminum sulfate and hydrogen gas are produced. If you need to produce 30 moles of aluminum sulfate, will 400 grams of aluminum be enough? Show proof of your answer with calculations.

$$\underline{2Al} + 3H_2(SO_4) \longrightarrow \underline{Al_2(SO_4)_3} + 3H_2$$
ha2:1 ratio

To produce 30 moles of aluminum sulfate, we'd need 60 moles of aluminum. One mole of aluminum has a mass of 27 grams. 60 x 27 grams = **1620 grams would be required. 400 grams of aluminum would not be enough!**

Name _____ Date _____
Friendly Chemistry

Lesson 25 Test
Do I Have Enough Reactant?

Read each problem below carefully. Find the necessary amount of ingredient to produce the desired amount of product. Take your time and ask questions if needed.

1. Marcus needed to prepare 50 moles of lead. He knew that if he mixed lead (II) nitrate with zinc, he could produce zinc nitrate and lead. How many moles of lead (II) nitrate would be necessary to make the 50 moles of lead?

    *Here is our reaction: $\underline{Pb(NO_3)_2}$ + Zn —> $Zn(NO_3)_2$ + $\underline{Pb}$; Mole ratio id 1:1.
    If Marcus needs to prepare 50 moles of lead,
    it will require **50 moles of lead (II) nitrate**.*

2. Francine read that when iron (III) nitrate was mixed with lithium hydroxide, iron (III) hydroxide and lithium nitrate are produced. If Francine needed to prepare 13 moles of iron (III) hydroxide, how many **grams** of lithium hydroxide would she need?

    *Here is our reaction: $Fe(NO_3)_3$ + $\underline{3Li(OH)}$ —> $\underline{Fe(OH)_3}$ + $3Li(NO_3)$; Mole ratio is 3:1.
    If Francine needs to prepare 13 moles of iron (III) hydroxide, based on the mole ratio,
    she will need 39 moles of lithium hydroxide (3 x 13).
    We've been asked to determine how many grams of lithium hydroxide she needs, so we
    need to convert this result into grams. One mole of lithium hydroxide has a formula
    weight of 24 grams. 39 moles x 24 grams per mole = **936 grams lithium hydroxide**.*

3. Tony knew that water could be separated into its components: hydrogen gas and oxygen gas. If Tony needed to prepare 400 moles of hydrogen gas, how many **grams** of water would he need to accomplish this task?

    *Here is our reaction: $\underline{2H_2O}$ —> $\underline{2H_2}$ + O_2; Mole ratio is 1:1
    If Tony needs to make 400 moles of hydrogen gas, he'll need to have 400 moles of water. One mole of water has a formula weight of 18 grams. 400 moles x 18 grams per mole =
    7200 grams of water will be needed.*

4. Marcia was told to prepare 210 grams of zinc sulfate. She knew that she could do this by using the reaction where zinc is mixed with sulfuric acid to produce zinc sulfate and hydrogen gas. How many **grams** of zinc would she need for this reaction in order to produce the 210 **grams** of zinc sulfate?

Here is our reaction: $\underline{Zn}$ + $H_2(SO_4)$ —> $\underline{Zn(SO_4)}$ + H_2; Mole ratio is 1:1
Marcia has been asked to prepare 210 grams of zinc sulfate. First, we need to convert this amount into moles in order to apply the mole ratio. One mole of zinc sulfate has a formula weight of 161 grams. 210 grams / 161 grams per mole = 1.3 moles. So, Marcia needs to prepare 1.3 moles of zinc sulfate. Now, we can apply the mole ratio: in order to prepare 1.3 moles of zinc sulfate, Marcia will need 1.3 moles of zinc. We need to know how many grams of zinc she will need, so we need to convert this last result into grams. One mole of zinc weighs 65 grams.
*1.3 moles x 65 grams per mole = **84.5 grams of zinc.***

5. When barium chloride is mixed with potassium bromide, potassium chloride, barium and bromine gas are produced (barium chloride + potassium bromide yields potassium chloride, barium and bromine gas). You have been asked to prepare 500 grams of potassium chloride from this reaction. Will you have enough barium chloride if your stock container says you have 500 grams available? Show proof of your work. Note that bromine gas is a diatomic gas.

Here is our reaction: $\underline{BaCl_2}$ + 2KBr —> $\underline{2KCl}$ + Ba + Br_2; Mole ratio is 1:2
*We need to prepare 500 grams of KCl. Let's convert that to moles in order to apply the mole ratio. One mole of KCl has a formula weight of 74 grams. 500 grams / 74 grams per mole = 6.7 moles. We can now apply the mole ratio: in order to prepare 6.7 moles of KCl, we will need 3.35 moles of $BaCl_2$. Let's convert this result back into grams to see if we have enough available in our stock container. One mole of $BaCl_2$ has a formula weight of 207 grams. We need 3.35 moles of it, so 3.35 moles x 207 grams = **693 grams $BaCl_2$. Our stock container has 500 grams, therefore, we won't have enough.***

6. Terry took 50 grams of iron and dropped it into copper (II) sulfate. Iron (II) sulfate and copper were produced. How many grams of copper did he yield from his 50 grams of iron?
Here is our reaction: $\underline{Fe}$ + $Cu(SO_4)$ —> $Fe(SO_4)$ + $\underline{Cu}$; Mole ratio is 1:1
*Terry began with 50 grams of iron. Let's convert that amount into moles in order to apply the mole ratio. One mole of iron has a mass of 56 grams. 50 g / 56 grams per mole = 0.89 moles. We can now apply the mole ratio: 0.89 moles of Fe will produce 0.89 moles of copper. We've been asked to find out how many grams of copper Terry could produce. One mole of copper has a mass of 64 grams. 0.89 moles x 64 grams per mole = **56.96 grams of copper.***

Name_____ Date_____
Friendly Chemistry

Lesson 26: Preparing Solutions –1

Read each problem below. Work slowly and carefully.

1. Tony was asked to prepare a 3 M potassium chloride solution. How many grams of potassium chloride does Tony need?

   One mole of KCl has a mass of 74 grams.
   A 3M solution would have 3 x 74 grams = **222 grams**

2. Francis needed to prepare a 5.5 M sodium sulfate solution. How many grams of sodium sulfate does she need?

   One mole of $Na_2(SO_4)$ has a mass of 142 grams.
   A 5.5 M solution would have 5.5 x 146 grams = **781 grams**.

3. Harry was told to make a 0.5 M solution of nickel chromate. How many grams does of nickel chromate does Harry need?

   One mole of $Ni(CrO_4)$ has a mass of 175 grams.
   A 0.5 M solution would have 0.5 x 175 grams = **87.5 grams**

4. If you needed to prepare 2 liters of a 6 M calcium carbonate solution, how many grams of calcium carbonate do you need?

   One mole of $Ca(CO_3)$ has a weight of 100 grams. A 6 M solution would require 6 x 100 grams = 600 grams. This would be enough to make 1 liter. To make the desired 2 liters, it would take **1200 grams** *of calcium carbonate.*

5. Shorty needed to prepare 10 liters of a 4 M lithium acetate solution. How many grams of lithium acetate does he need?

One mole of $Li(C_2H_3O_2)$ has a mass of 66 grams. A 4 M solution would require 4 x 66 grams = 264 grams. To make 10 liters of this solution, it would require 10 x 264 grams = **2640 grams of lithium acetate**.

6. Lisa was asked to prepare 0.5 liters of a 2 M iron (III) chloride solution. How many grams of iron (III) chloride does she need?

One mole of $FeCl_3$ has a mass of 161 grams.
A 2M solution would require 2 x 161 grams = 322 grams.
0.5 liters would require 322 x 0.5 = **161 grams iron (III) chloride**.

7. Tommy used 513 grams of calcium phosphate to prepare one liter of solution. What was the molarity of this solution?

One mole of $Ca_3(PO_4)_2$ has a mass of 310 grams. Tommy used 513 grams. We need to find out how many moles Tommy used. 513 grams/310 grams per mole = 1.65 moles. He used this in 1 liter, therefore Tommy made a **1.65M solution**.

8. Sherry added 720 grams of copper (II) sulfite to one liter of water. What was the molarity of the solution she made?

One mole of $Cu(SO_3)$ has a mass of 144 grams. If Sherry used 720 grams, she used 720/144 grams per mole = 5 moles. Since she added these 5 moles to one liter of water, she made a **5M solution**.

Friendly Chemistry

Name_____   Date_____

Friendly Chemistry

Lesson 26: Preparing Solutions –2

1. Frank needed to make 4 liters of a 3 M potassium permanganate solution. How much potassium permanganate does Frank need?

    One mole of K(MnO₄) has a mass of 158 grams.
    A 3M solution would require 3 x 158 grams = 474 grams.
    Four liters of this solution would require 4 x 474 grams = **1896 grams**

2. Trish had 294 grams of copper (II) hydroxide. If she added this to 1 liter of solvent, what would the resulting molarity of the solution be?

    One mole of Cu(OH)₂ has a mass of 98 grams. Trish used 294 grams which is equal To 294/98 grams per mole = 3 moles. As this was added to one liter of solvent, the resulting solution would be **3M**.

3. Dan was asked to prepare 10 liters of a 0.1 M hydrogen chloride solution. How many grams of hydrogen chloride does he need?

    One mole of HCl has a mass of 36 grams.
    A 0.1 M solution would use 0.1 x 36 grams = 3.6 grams per liter of solvent.
    10 liters would require **36 grams of HCl**.

4. Toni put 35 grams of barium iodide into 1 liter of water. What was the resulting molarity of the solution?

    One mole of BaI₂ has a mass of 391 grams.
    35 grams represents 35/391 grams per mole = 0.09 moles.
    Since Toni added this amount to one liter of water, she made a **0.09M solution**.

5. Billy put 360 grams of calcium sulfite into one liter of water. What was the molarity of the resulting solution?

    One mole Ca(SO₃) has a mass of 120 grams.
    360 grams represents 360/120 grams per mole = 3 moles.
    Since Billy added these 3 moles to one liter of water, he created a **3M solution**.

6. Charlotte and Perry were each asked to prepare a 0.6 M solution of magnesium cyanide. Charlotte said they needed 45.6 grams. Perry said they needed 76 grams. Who was correct? Or were they both wrong? Show proof of your answer.

One mole of $Mg(CN)_2$ has a mass of 76 grams. They were asked to prepare a 0.6M solution. So, 0.6 x 76 grams per mole = 45.6 grams.
Charlotte was correct!

7. Antonio was asked to prepare a 17.5 M ammonium hypochlorite solution. How many grams of the compound should he get?

One mole of $(NH_4)(ClO)$ has a mass of 69 grams.
A 17.5 M solution would have 17.5 x 69 grams = **1207.5 grams**.

8. Sheila told Tom she was going to make a 0.1 M sodium chloride solution. She said she needed to get 5.8 grams of sodium chloride. Was she correct? Show proof with calculations.

One mole of NaCl has a mass of 58 grams. A 0.1 M solution would have 0.1 x 58 grams = **5.8 grams** *per liter of solvent.* **Sheila was correct**.

NAME_____ DATE_____
FRIENDLY CHEMISTRY

Lesson 26 Test
Molarity

1. Frank needed to make 2.5 liters of a 1.0 M potassium permanganate solution. How much potassium permanganate does Frank need?

   A 1.0 M solution has 1 mole of potassium permanganate per liter of solution. One mole of K(Mn)$_4$ has a formula weight of 158 grams. Therefore, one liter would require 158 grams. 2.5 liters would require 2.5 x 158 g = **395 grams**.

2. Tina had 637 grams of copper (II) hydroxide. If she added this compound to 1 liter of solvent, what would the resulting molarity of the solution be?

   We need to determine how many moles of Cu(OH)$_2$ Tina has. One mole of Cu(OH)$_2$ has a formula weight of 97 grams. 637 g / 97 grams per mole = 6.5 moles. Tina has added this amount to one liter of solvent, therefore she has a **6.5 M solution**.

3. Derek was asked to prepare 3 liters of a 0.2 M hydrogen chloride solution. How many grams of hydrogen chloride does he need?

   Hydrogen chloride, HCl, has a formula weight of 36 grams. A 0.2 M solution would have 0.2 x 36 grams = 7.2 grams of HCl per liter of solvent. Derek needs to prepare 3 liters, therefore, 3 x 7.2 grams = **21.6 grams HCl**.

4. Toni put 35 grams of barium iodide into 1 liter of water. What was the resulting molarity of the solution?

   BaI$_2$ has a formula weight of 391 grams. 35 g / 391 grams per mole = **.09 M solution**.

5. Josephine was asked to prepare 2 liters of a 6 M calcium carbonate solution. How many grams of calcium carbonate will she need?

$Ca(CO_3)$ has a formula weight of 100 grams.
A 6M solution would have 6 x 100 grams per liter = 600 grams.
*Josephine needs 2 liters of this solution, therefore, 2 x 600 grams = **1200 grams**.*

6. Mark took 480 grams of calcium and added it to one liter of solvent. What was the molarity of his solution?

*One mole of Ca has a mass of 40 grams. 480 grams / 40 grams per mole = 12 moles. Since Mark added this to one liter of solvent, he has prepared a **12 M solution**.*

7. Sara and Tim were asked to prepare a 3 M solution of barium nitrite. Sara calculated that they would need 783 grams. Tim said they would need 687 grams. Who was correct or were they both wrong? Show proof of your answer.

$Ba(NO_2)_2$ has a formula weight of 229 grams.
*A 3M solution would have 3 x 229 grams = **687 grams**.*
***Tim was correct**.*

Apparently Sara wrote the compound formula as $Ba(**NO_3**)_2$ which has a formula weight of 261 grams. 3 x 261 g = 783 grams.

8. Margot took 5 moles of sodium chloride and added it to 2 liters of water. What was the resulting molarity of the solution she made?

*5 moles of NaCl added to 2 liters of water would be the same as 2.5 moles added to 1 liter of water. Therefore, Margot created a **2.5M solution** of NaCl and water.*

9. When hot chocolate powder is mixed with hot water to make hot cocoa, which component is identified as being the solvent?
***Hot water is the solvent**.*

10. Regarding the information in question #9, which component is the solute?

The hot chocolate powder is the solute.

Name_____ Date_____
Friendly Chemistry

Lesson 27: Stoichiometry Problems –1
Beginning with Milliliters of Solutions

Read each problem below. Work slowly and carefully.

1. Jenny had 45 mls of a 2 M sodium hydroxide solution. If she mixed all 45 mls of this solution with hydrogen chloride, how many grams of sodium chloride could she produce from this reaction. Water is a byproduct of the reaction.

Our reaction is: Na(OH) + HCl —> NaCl + H(OH) and is balanced as written. We need to determine how many grams Jenny is starting with. She is using a 2 M sodium hydroxide solution. One mole of Na(OH) has a mass of 40 grams. A 2M solution would therefore have 80 grams per liter or 80 grams/1000 ml.
So, we can set-up this relationship:

$$\frac{80 \text{ grams}}{1000 \text{ ml}} = \frac{x \text{ grams}}{45 \text{ ml}}$$

X = 3.36 grams. So, Jenny is beginning the reaction with 3.6 grams of Na(OH). We need to convert this result into moles. 3.6 grams / 40 grams per mole = 0.09 moles We can now apply the mole ratio: 1:1.
0.09 moles of Na(OH) will yield 0.09 moles NaCl.
The question asks for grams of NaCl. So, we need to convert our 0.09 moles NaCl to grams. One mole of NaCl has a mass of 58 grams. 0.09 moles x 58 grams = 5.22 grams
So, Jenny produced 5.22 grams of NaCl from her 45 mls of 2M Na(OH) solution.

2. Tony knew that ammonia (NH_3) will react with hydrogen sulfide to produce ammonium sulfide. If Tony had 100 mls of a 0.5 M ammonia solution, how many grams of ammonium sulfide could he potentially produce from this reaction? Assume Tony used all 100 mls of ammonia.

Our reaction is: <u>$2NH_3$</u> *+ H_2S —>* <u>$(NH_4)_2S$</u> *A 2:1 ratio.*
Let's look a what Tony started with: 100 mls of a 0.5 M solution. One mole of ammonia has a mass of 17 grams. A 0.5M solution would therefore contain 8.5 grams per one liter or 8.5 grams / 1000 mls. We can set-up this relationship:

$$\frac{8.5 \text{ grams}}{1000 \text{ mls}} = \frac{x \text{ grams}}{100 \text{ mls}}$$

X = 0.85 grams.
So Tony was starting the reaction with 0.85 grams of ammonia. We need to convert this result into moles. One mole of ammonia = 17 grams, therefore, Tony began the reaction with 0.85 grams / 17 grams per mole = .05 moles.
We can now apply the mole ratio: .05 moles of ammonia will yield 0.025 moles of $(NH_4)_2S$
Let's convert this result back into grams. One mole of $(NH_4)_2S$ has a mass of 68 grams. 0.025 moles would equal 0.025 x 68 = ***1.7 grams***.

3. Julie had 50 mls of 5 M copper (II) sulfate. If she combined this compound with iron filings (shavings of iron metal), she could produce iron (II) sulfate and copper. How many grams of copper cold she potentially produce is she used all 50 mls of the 5M copper (II) sulfate solution?

Our reaction is: $Cu(SO_4)$ + Fe —> $Fe(SO_4)$ + Cu Mole ratio is 1:1.
Julie begins with 50 mls of a 5M solution. One mole of $Cu(SO_4)$ has a mass of 160 grams. A 5 M solution would have 5 x 160 g/L = 800 grams/L. She is using 50 mls, so we can set up this relationship:

$$\frac{800 \text{ g}}{1000 \text{ ml}} = \frac{x \text{ g}}{50 \text{ ml}}$$

X = 40 grams, so Julie is beginning her reaction with 40 grams of $Cu(SO_4)$.
Let's convert this result to moles. 40 grams/160 grams per mole = 0.25 moles
Apply the mole ratio: 0.25 moles of $Cu(SO_4)$ will yield 0.25 moles of Cu.
One mole of copper has a mass of 64 grams, therefore, 0.25 x 64 grams = **16 grams of copper.**

4. Leroy took 1 liter of 0.25 M potassium chlorate and allowed it to decompose into potassium chloride and oxygen gas. How many grams of potassium chloride could you predict he generated from this reaction?

Our reaction is $2K(ClO_3)$ —> $2KCl$ + $3O_2$ Mole ratio is 1:1.
Leroy begins with 1 L of a 0.25M $K(ClO_3)$ solution. One mole of $K(ClO_3)$ has a mass of 122 grams. A 0.25M solution would have 0.25 x 122 grams per L = 30.5 grams per L.

If Leroy used the whole liter, he would be using 30.5 grams in his reaction. Let's convert this result into moles in order to apply the mole ratio: 30.5 grams/122 grams per mole = 0.25 moles.
We can now apply the mole ratio: 0.25 moles of $K(ClO_3)$ will yield 0.25 moles of KCl. Finally, let's convert this result back into grams. One mole of KCl has a mass of 74 grams. 0.25 moles x 74 grams per mole = **18.5 grams KCl.**

Friendly Chemistry

Name_____ Date_____
Friendly Chemistry

Lesson 27: Stoichiometry Problems –2
Beginning with Milliliters of Solutions

Read each problem below. Work slowly and carefully.

1. When zinc coated bolts are dropped into sulfuric acid (hydrogen sulfate), zinc sulfate and hydrogen gas are produced. Suppose Tim dropped some of these bolts into 200 mls of 2.0 M sulfuric acid. How many grams of zinc sulfate did he produce from this reaction?

    Here is our reaction: $Zn + \underline{H_2(SO_4)} \longrightarrow \underline{Zn(SO_4)} + H_2$ 1:1 ratio
    Tim began with 200 ml of 2.0 M $H_2(SO_4)$. One mole of $H_2(SO_4)$ has a mass of 98 grams. A 2M solution will have 2 x 98 grams per liter = 196 grams per liter. Tim used 200 ml of this solution. We can create the following relationship:

    $$\frac{196\ g}{1000\ ml} = \frac{x\ g}{200\ ml}$$

    $X = 39.2\ grams$

    So, Tim is beginning his reaction with 39.2 grams of $H_2(SO_4)$.
    Let's convert this result to moles in order to apply the mole ratio. 1 mole of $H_2(SO_4)$ has a mass 98 grams. 39.2 / 98 grams = 0.4 moles
    We can now apply the mole ratio: 0.4 moles of $H_2(SO_4)$ will produce 0.4 moles of $Zn(SO_4)$. Now we just need to convert this result back into grams.
    One mole of $Zn(SO_4)$ has a mass of 161 grams. 0.4 moles of $Zn(SO_4)$ x 161 grams per mole = **64.4 grams $Zn(SO_4)$.**

2. Potassium perchlorate decomposes into potassium chloride and oxygen gas. If you begin with 50 mls of a 12 M potassium perchlorate solution, how many grams of potassium chloride might you produce from this reaction?

    Our reaction is $\underline{K(ClO_4)} \longrightarrow \underline{KCl} + 2O_2$ Mole ratio is 1:1.
    We are beginning with 50 mls of a 12 M solution. First, lets find out how many grams are in one liter of the solution. One mole of $K(ClO_4)$ has a mass of 138 grams. A 12 M solution would have 12 x 138 grams = 1656 grams per liter of solution.
    We are beginning with 50 mls of this solution. Let's set up this relationship:

    $$\frac{1656\ g}{1000\ mls} = \frac{X\ grams}{50\ mls}$$

    $X = 82.8\ grams$

    So, we are beginning with 82.8 grams of $K(ClO_4)$. We'll need to convert this to moles next. One mole of $K(ClO_4)$ has a formula weight of 138 grams. 82.8 grams/138 grams per mole = 0.6 moles. We can now apply the mole ratio. Our 0.6 moles of $K(ClO_4)$ will produce 0.6 moles of KCl. We'll need to convert this result back to grams. One mole of KCl has a formula weight of 74 grams. 0.6 m x 74 grams per moles = **44.4 grams KCl.**

3. 400 mls of a 1.5 M iron (III) nitrate solution were mixed with lithium hydroxide. Iron (III) hydroxide and lithium nitrate were produced. How many grams of each product were made?

Our first reaction is: $\underline{Fe(NO_3)_3}$ + 3Li(OH) —> $\underline{Fe(OH)_3}$ + 3Li(NO_3); 1:1 ratio

A 1.5 M $Fe(NO_3)_3$ solution will have 1.5 moles per liter. $Fe(NO_3)_3$ has a formula weight of 242 grams. Therefore a 1.5 M solution will have 1.5 x 242 g per liter = 363 grams per liter solution. We are beginning with 400 mls. We can make this relationship:

$$\frac{363\ g}{1000\ mls} = \frac{X\ g}{400\ mls}$$

$$X = 145.2\ grams$$

Let's convert this result to moles and then apply the mole ratio. 145.2 grams/242 g per mole = 0.6 moles. By applying the mole ratio, we find that 0.6 moles of $Fe(NO_3)_3$ will yield 0.6 moles of $Fe(OH)_3$.

Now, we just need to convert this result back into grams of this product. One mole of $Fe(OH)_3$ has a formula weight of 107 grams. 0.6 moles x 107 grams =
64.2 grams $Fe(OH)_3$

For the second product, we'll obviously use the same reaction, but have a different mole ratio. Here's the reaction, again:
$\underline{Fe(NO_3)_3}$ + 3Li(OH) —> $Fe(OH)_3$ + $\underline{3Li(NO_3)}$; 1:3 ratio

From our work above, we know that we are beginning with 0.6 moles of iron (III) nitrate. Let's apply the new mole ratio: 0.6 moles of iron (III) nitrate will produce 1.8 moles of lithium nitrate. Let's convert this result back to grams. One mole of lithium nitrate has a mass of 69 grams. 1.8 m x 69 grams/mole =
124.2 +/- grams lithium nitrate.

4. Tony had 5 moles of sodium acetate. Mary had 5 moles of barium acetate. Who had the most atoms? Show your work.

Ahh...a trick question!
Tony had 5 moles. Mary has 5 moles.
We know that one mole of ANY element has 6.02×10^{23} atoms. Since each has the same number of moles (5), **they must both have the same number of atoms**!

NAME_____ DATE_____

FRIENDLY CHEMISTRY

Lesson 27 Test
Molarity in Stoichiometry Problems

1. Tommy had 200 mls of a 2 M hydrogen cyanide solution. Into this solution he poured in some sodium sulfate. Hydrogen sulfate and sodium cyanide were produced by the reaction. How many grams of sodium cyanide did he produce?

$2HCN + Na_2(SO_4) \longrightarrow H_2(SO_4) + 2NaCN$; 1:1 ratio

A 2 M solution has two moles per liter. One mole of HCN = 27 grams. 2 x 27 grams per liter = 54 grams per liter. Set up the relationship:

$$\frac{54 \text{ grams}}{1000 \text{ mls}} = \frac{X \text{ grams}}{200 \text{ mls}}$$

$X = 10.8$ grams.

We need to convert this into moles: 10.8 g / 27 grams per mole = 0.4 moles. Apply the mole ratio: 0.4 moles of HCN will produce 0.4 moles of NaCN. One mole of NaCN = 49 grams.

0.4 moles x 49 g/mole = **19.6 grams NaCN**

2. Terry took magnesium and mixed it with some hydrochloric acid. Magnesium chloride and hydrogen gas were produced by the reaction that took place. If he used 100 mls of a 6 M hydrochloric acid with excess magnesium, how many grams of magnesium chloride was produced by the reaction?

$Mg + 2HCl \longrightarrow MgCl_2 + H_2$; 2:1 mole ratio

A 6 M HCl solution will have 6 moles of HCl per liter of solvent. One mole of HCl = 36 grams. 6 x 36 grams per liter = 216 grams per liter of solution. We can setup the following relationship:

$$\frac{216 \text{ grams}}{1000 \text{ mls}} = \frac{X \text{ grams}}{100 \text{ mls}}$$

$X = 21.6$ grams

Let's convert this into moles in order to apply the mole ratio.
21.6 grams / 36 grams per mole = 0.6 moles.
Applying the mole ratio: 0.6 moles of HCl will produce 0.3 moles of $MgCl_2$.
0.3 moles of $MgCl_2$ x 94 grams per mole = **28.2 grams $MgCl_2$.**

3. Barium oxide and carbon dioxide react to produce barium carbonate. Jane took 900 mls of a 7 M barium oxide solution and allowed the carbon dioxide to bubble through it. How many grams of barium carbonate did she produce if all of the barium oxide was used in the reaction?

$BaO + CO_2 \rightarrow Ba(CO_3)$; 1:1 mole ratio.

A 7M BaO solution will have 7 moles per liter. One mole of BaO has a formula weight of 153 grams. 7 x 153 grams per mole = 1071 grams per liter (1000 mls).
We can setup this relationship:

$$\frac{1071 g}{1000 \text{ mls}} = \frac{X g}{900 \text{ mls}}$$

$$X = 963.9 \text{ grams}$$

We need to convert this result into moles in order to apply the mole ratio. 963.9 g / 153 grams per mole = 6.3 moles. Applying the mole ratio we see that 6.3 moles of BaO will produce 6.3 moles of $Ba(CO_3)$. One mole of $Ba(CO_3)$ has a formula weight of 197 grams. 6.3 moles x 197 grams per mole = **1241.1 grams**.

4. Iron (III) nitrate and lithium hydroxide react to yield iron (III) hydroxide and lithium nitrate. If you began with 500 mls of a 3.5 M lithium hydroxide solution, how many grams of lithium nitrate could you produce from this reaction?

$Fe(NO_3)_3 + 3Li(OH) \rightarrow Fe(OH)_3 + 3Li(NO_3)$; 1:1 mole ratio.

A 3.5 M Li(OH) solution will have 3.5 moles of lithium hydroxide per 1 liter of solvent. One mole Li(OH) has a formula weight of 24 grams. 3.5 moles x 24 grams per mole = 84 grams per liter (1000 mls) solvent.
We can setup the following relationship:

$$\frac{84 \text{ grams}}{1000 \text{ mls}} = \frac{X \text{ grams}}{500 \text{ mls}}$$

$$X = 42 \text{ grams}$$

We need to convert this result into moles in order to apply the mole ratio. 42 grams / 24 grams per mole = 1.75 moles. Applying the mole ratio, we find that 1.75 moles of Li(OH) will produce 1.75 moles of $Li(NO_3)$.
One mole of $Li(NO_3)$ has a formula weight of 69 grams.
1.75 moles x 69 grams per mole = **120.75 grams $Li(NO_3)$**.

5. Magnesium chlorate will decompose to produce magnesium chloride and oxygen gas. If you began with 2.5 L of a 2 M magnesium chlorate solution, how many grams of magnesium chloride could you produce from this reaction?

$Mg(ClO_3)_2 \rightarrow MgCl_2 + 3O_2$; 1:1 mole ratio.

A 2 M $Mg(ClO_3)_2$ solution will have 2 moles $Mg(ClO_3)_2$ per liter (1000 mls) of solvent. One mole of $Mg(ClO_3)_2$ has a formula weight of 190 grams.
2 moles x 190 grams per mole = 380 grams per 1000 mls of solution.
We can setup the following relationship:

$$\frac{380 \text{ grams}}{1000 \text{ mls}} = \frac{X \text{ grams}}{2500 \text{ mls}}$$

$$X = 950 \text{ grams}$$

We need to convert this result into moles in order to apply the mole ratio. 950 grams / 190 grams per mole = 5 moles $Mg(ClO_3)_2$. Applying the mole ratio, we see that 5 moles of $Mg(ClO_3)_2$ will produce 5 moles $MgCl_2$. One mole of $MgCl_2$ has a formula weight of 94 grams. 5 moles x 94 grams per mole = **470 grams $MgCl_2$**.

Name_____ Date_____
Friendly Chemistry

Lesson 28: Molarity Problems –1
Determining Volume of Reactant Necessary to Produce Desired Product

Read each problem below. Work slowly and carefully. Ask if you have questions.

1. Joe has been asked to prepare 300 grams of hydrogen cyanide for his boss. He is going to use the following reaction: Hydrogen sulfate and sodium cyanide react to yield hydrogen cyanide and sodium sulfate. He has 3 M hydrogen sulfate on hand for the reaction. How many milliliters of this solution will be required to make the 300 grams of H(CN)?

Here's our reaction: $\underline{H_2(SO_4)}$ + 2NaCN —> $\underline{2HCN}$ + $Na_2(SO_4)$; 1:2 ratio

Joe needs to make 300 grams of HCN. Let's convert this into moles first so we can apply the mole ratio. One mole of HCN has a formula weight of 27 grams. 300 grams/27 grams per mole = 11.1 moles. So Joe needs to prepare 11.1 moles.

Let's apply the mole ratio now: To prepare 11.1 moles it will require half that amount of hydrogen sulfate which would be 5.5 moles.

We need to look at the solution Joe has on hand to prepare this product. It's a 3 M solution and he needs 5.5 moles. Let's set up this relationship:

From a 3M soluntion, you get 3 moles in 1000 ml, so how many mls will it take to get 5.5 moles? Mathematically, this relationship looks like this:

$$\frac{3 \text{ moles}}{1000 \text{ mls}} = \frac{5.5 \text{ moles}}{X \text{ mls}}$$

Solving for X, we get X = 1833 mls.

So, Joe would need 1833 mls to make the desired 300 grams of HCN.

(Note: if you found you needed to use 5.55 moles of HCN (you didn't round), your final answer will be 1850 grams). No sweat—either response works!

2. Patricia was preparing to make 450 grams of zinc chloride. She knew that when zinc oxide and hydrochloric acid are combined, they product zinc chloride and water. She looked on her supply shelf and found she had 5 M hydrochloric acid and plenty of zinc oxide. How many milliliters of the 5 M hydrochloric acid will she need?

Here's our reaction: ZnO + $\underline{2HCl}$ —> $\underline{ZnCl_2}$ + H_2O; 2:1 ratio

Patricia needs to prepare 450 g of $ZnCl_2$. Let's convert that into moles in order to apply the mole ratio. One mole of $ZnCl_2$ has a formula weight of 135 g. 450g/135 g per mole = 3.3 moles of $ZnCl_2$. We can now apply the mole ratio: in order to prepare 3.33 moles of $ZnCl_2$ we would need 6.6 moles of HCl.

Pat's solution is 5M HCl which means there are 5 moles of HCl per liter of water. Let's set up this relationship: if we know we can get 5 moles of HCl in 1000 ml of solution, how many mls of this solution will it take to get 6.6 moles of HCl? Mathematically, this relationship would look like this:

$$\frac{5 \text{ moles}}{1000 \text{ mls}} = \frac{6.6 \text{ moles}}{X \text{ mls}}$$

X= 1320 mls

3. Terry knew that carbon and aluminum oxide will react to produce aluminum and carbon dioxide. If Terry had a container of 5 M aluminum oxide in his supply cupboard, how many milliliters would it take for him to prepare 500 grams of aluminum based upon his reaction?

Here's our reaction: $3C + \underline{2Al_2O_3} \longrightarrow \underline{4Al} + 3CO_2$; 2:4 or 1:2 ratio.
Terry wants to make 500 grams of Al. Let's see how many moles that is equal to so that we can then apply the mole ratio. One mole of Al weighs 27 grams, therefore 500/27 grams per mole = 18.5 moles. We can now apply the mole ratio. In order to make 18.5 moles of Al, we'd need 9.25 moles of Al_2O_3.
Terry's solution of aluminum oxide was 5M which means there are 5 moles of aluminum oxide in every 1000 mls of solution. Let's set up this relationship: if you can get 5 moles of aluminum oxide in 1000 mls of solution, how many mls of solution will it take to get 9.25 moles? Mathematically, this relationship looks like this:

$$\frac{5\ m}{1000\ mls} = \frac{9.25\ m}{X\ mls}$$
$$X = 1850\ mls.$$

So, Terry would need 1850 mls of his solution.

4. Martha read that iron (III) nitrate and lithium hydroxide would undergo a double replacement reaction to produce iron (III) hydroxide and lithium nitrate. If Martha took 100 mls of a 3.5 M lithium hydroxide solution, how many grams of lithium nitrate could she expect to produce?

$Fe(NO_3)_3 + \underline{3Li(OH)} \longrightarrow Fe(OH)_3 + \underline{3Li(NO_3)}$; 3:3 or 1:1 ratio.
Note this problem asks for what we can produce from the reaction, not how much it will take as we were asked for in the three previous problems.
Martha has 100 mls of a 3.5 M solution. First, let's see how many grams she has, then convert that into moles in order to apply the mole ratio.
First we need to find the formula weight of lithium hydroxide which is 24 grams. A 3.5 M solution will therefore have 3.5 x 24 grams = 84 grams present in 1 liter of solution. Martha has 100 mls of this solution. So, let's set up our relationship as follows:

$$\frac{84\ grams}{1000\ mls} = \frac{X\ grams}{100\ mls}$$
$$X = 8.4\ grams$$

This means that Martha is starting her reaction with 8.4 grams lithium hydroxide. Now, we'll need to convert this result into moles in order to apply the mole ratio. One mole of lithium hydroxide has a mass of 24 grams (found above). So, 8.4/24 grams per mole = 0.35 moles Li(OH).
Now, we can apply the mole ratio:
0.35 moles of Li(OH) will produce 0.35 moles of $Li(NO_3)$. We have been asked to see how many grams of lithium nitrate we will produce, so we'll need to convert our current answer into grams. One mole of $Li(NO_3)$ has a formula weight of 69 grams. So 0.35 moles x 69 grams per mole = **24.15 grams lithium nitrate.**

Name_____ Date_____
Friendly Chemistry

Lesson 28: Molarity Problems –2
Determining Volume of Reactant Necessary to Produce Desired Product

Read each problem below. Work slowly and carefully.

1. When zinc is placed into sulfuric acid (hydrogen sulfate), zinc sulfate and hydrogen gas are produced. Suppose you needed to produce 1000 grams of zinc sulfate from this reaction. You had plenty of zinc on hand and found you had 750 milliliters of 6 M sulfuric acid available for use. Would you have enough? Show your work as proof of your answer.

Our reaction is: $Zn + \underline{H_2(SO_4)} \longrightarrow \underline{Zn(SO_4)} + H_2$; 1:1 ratio.
We need to produce 1000 grams of zinc sulfate. Let's convert this to moles in order to apply the mole ratio. One mole of zinc sulfate has a formula weight of 161 grams. 1000 grams/ 161 grams per mole = 6.2 moles. We can now apply the mole ratio: to make the desired 6.2 moles of zinc sulfate, it will require 6.2 moles of hydrogen sulfate. Now, lets look at the solution of hydrogen sulfate we have available. It's a 6 M solution which means that there are 6 moles of hydrogen sulfate per liter of solution. We can set-up this relationship:

$$\frac{6 \text{ moles } H_2(SO_4)}{1000 \text{ mls}} = \frac{6.2 \text{ moles } H_2(SO_4)}{X \text{ mls}}$$

$$X = 1033 \text{ mls}$$

Based upon these results, we see that in order to make the desired 1000 grams of zinc sulfate, we would need 1033 milliliters of 6M hydrogen sulfate.
The 750 mls you have on hand would, therefore, not be enough!

2. Potassium perchlorate decomposes into potassium chloride and oxygen gas. If you have instructions of prepare 1 kilogram of potassium chloride for a lab activity, how many milliliters of a 0.5 M potassium perchlorate solution would you need?

Here is our reaction: $\underline{K(ClO_4)} \longrightarrow \underline{KCl} + 2O_2$ 1:1 ratio
We've been asked to prepare 1 kilogram of potassium chloride. One kilogram = 1000 grams. Let's convert that to moles first in order to apply the mole ratio. One mole of potassium chloride has a formula weight of 74 grams. 1000 g / 74 grams per mole = 13.5 moles. We can now apply the mole ratio: in order to prepare 13.5 moles of potassium chloride, we would need 13.5 moles of potassium perchlorate. Let's look at the solution we have: it's a 0.5 M solution which means there is 0.5 moles per liter (1000mls) solution. We can set up this relationship:

$$\frac{0.5 \text{ moles}}{1000 \text{ mls}} = \frac{13.5 \text{ moles}}{X \text{ mls}}$$

$$X = 27{,}000 \text{ mls or } 27 \text{ liters}$$

*Therefore, in order to make the desired 1 kilogram of potassium chloride, you would need **27 liters of potassium perchlorate**.*

3. Trey needed to prepare 5 kg of sodium chloride from the reaction of hydrogen chloride and sodium hydroxide. If his hydrogen chloride solution was 2 M, how may milliliters would he need? Water is a byproduct of the reaction.

Here is our reaction: $\underline{HCl}$ + $Na(OH)$ —> $\underline{NaCl}$ + $H(OH)$; *mole ratio is 1:1*
Trey needs to prepare 5 kg of sodium chloride which is equal to 5000 grams (1 kg = 1000 g). Let's convert this amount into moles in order to apply the mole ratio. One mole of NaCl = 58 grams. 5000g / 58 grams per mole = 86.2 moles.
We can now apply the mole ratio. In order to prepare 86.2 moles of sodium chloride, we will need to have 86.2 moles of HCl.
Our solution is 2M meaning we get 2 moles of HCl per liter (1000 mls) of solution. We can set up this relationship:

$$\frac{2 \text{ moles HCl}}{1000 \text{ mls}} = \frac{86.2 \text{ moles HCl}}{X \text{ mls}}$$

X = 43,100 mls or 43.1 liters

4. Melissa had 500 ml of a 2 M barium oxide solution. If she bubbled carbon dioxide through this solution, how many grams of barium carbonate could she expect to produce?

Here is our reaction: $\underline{BaO}$ + CO_2 —> $\underline{Ba(CO_3)}$; *mole ratio is 1:1*
Melissa's solution is 2M which means there is 2 moles of BaO per 1000 mls of solution. She is using 500 mls of solution, so let's set up a relationship to determine the actual number of grams she is using. First, we'll need to find out how many grams of BaO is present in one mole. A formula weight calculation tells us that one mole of BaO has a weight of 153 grams. A 2M solution would have 2 x 153 grams per mole = 306 grams per liter (1000 mls) solution. Here is our relationship:

$$\frac{306 \text{ grams}}{1000 \text{ mls}} = \frac{X \text{ grams}}{500 \text{ mls}}$$

$$X = 153 \text{ grams}$$

So, Melissa is beginning with 153 grams of BaO. We'll need to convert this result in to moles in order to apply the mole ratio. One mole of BaO has a formula weight of 153 grams. So, 153 grams / 153 grams per mole = 1 mole BaO. In other words, Melissa is beginning her reaction with 1 mole of BaO. The mole ratio is 1:1, so from her one mole of BaO, she will produce 1 mole of Ba(CO$_3$). We've been asked to tell how many grams this is equal to, so we'll need a formula weight of Ba(CO$_3$). One mole of barium carbonate has a mass of 197 grams. **Based upon these results, we see that Melissa will produce 197 grams of barium carbonate from her 500 mls of 2M BaO solution.**

NAME_____ DATE_____
FRIENDLY CHEMISTRY

Lesson 28 Test
Determining Volume of Reactants Needed to Complete a Reaction

Read each problem below carefully. Follow the necessary steps to find the volume of reactant necessary to produce the desired amount of product.

1. Theresa knew that calcium and bromine gas reacted to yield calcium bromide. If Theresa needed to produce 10 moles of calcium bromide, how many milliliters of a 2 M calcium solution would she need?

   Here is our reaction: $Ca + Br_2 \longrightarrow CaBr_2$; Mole ratio is 1:1.
   Theresa needs to prepare 10 moles of calcium bromide. By applying the mole ratio, we can see that in order to prepare 10 moles of $CaBr_2$, we would need 10 moles of Ca. The calcium solution we are given is 2M meaning there are two moles of calcium in each liter (1000 mls) of solution. Based upon this, we can setup this relationship:

   $$\frac{2\ m\ Ca}{1000\ mls} = \frac{10\ m\ Ca}{X\ mls}$$

   X = 5000 mls or 5 liters 2M Ca.

2. Mark needed to prepare 310 grams of potassium fluoride. He knew he could do this by bubbling fluorine gas through a solution of potassium chloride. Chlorine gas is a byproduct of this reaction. How many milliliters of 5 M potassium chloride solution would he need in order to produce the desired 310 grams of potassium fluoride?

   Here is our reaction: $2KCl + F_2 \longrightarrow 2KF + Cl_2$; Mole ratio is 1:1.
   Mark needs to prepare 310 grams of KF. Let's convert this into moles in order to apply the mole ratio. One mole of KF has a formula weight of 58 grams. 310 / 58 grams per mole = 5.3 moles. Applying the mole ratio, we can say that in order to prepare 5.3 moles of KF, we would need 5.3 moles of KCl.
   The KCl solution that we have available is 5M. This means there are 5 moles of KCl in every 1 liter (1000 mls) of solution. Let's setup this relationship:

   $$\frac{5\ moles\ KCl}{1000\ mls} = \frac{5.3\ moles\ KCl}{X\ mls}$$

   X = 1060 mls 5 M KCl

3. Bruce had 100 mls of a 3M sodium hydroxide solution. He needed to make 500 grams of table salt (sodium chloride) from the reaction of sodium hydroxide and hydrochloric acid. Water is a byproduct of the reaction. Will he have enough sodium hydroxide to get the job done? Show proof of your answer.

Here is our reaction: Na(OH) + HCl —> NaCl + H(OH): Mole ratio is 1:1.
Bruce needs to prepare 500 grams of NaCl. Let's convert this amount into moles in order to apply the mole ratio. One mole of NaCl has a formula weight of 58 grams. 500 / 58 grams per mole = 8.6 moles NaCl.
We can apply the mole ratio now: in order to prepare 8.6 moles of NaCl, it will require 8.6 moles of Na(OH).
The solution Bruce has on hand is 3M. This means that within each liter, we'd find 3 moles of Na(OH). Let's setup this relationship to see exactly how many mls he will need:

$$\frac{3 \text{ moles}}{1000 \text{ mls}} = \frac{8.6 \text{ moles}}{X \text{ mls}}$$

X = 2866 mls
Bruce only has 100 mls, so he will not have enough to prepare the desired amount.

4. Ammonium carbonate decomposes to produce ammonia (NH_3), water and carbon dioxide. If Mary has 450 milliliters of a 5 M ammonium carbonate solution, how many grams of ammonia can you predict that she would yield from this reaction?

Here is our reaction: (NH$_4$)$_2$(CO$_3$) —> 2NH$_3$ + H$_2$O + CO$_2$; Mole ratio is 1:2.
Mary's solution is 5M which means she has 5 moles of ammonium carbonate in each liter of solution. One mole of ammonium carbonate has a formula weight of 96 grams.
5 moles x 96 grams per mole = 480 grams per 1000 mls of solution.
Knowing this, we can now setup this relationship:

$$\frac{480 \text{ grams}}{1000 \text{ mls}} = \frac{X \text{ grams}}{450 \text{ mls}}$$

X = 216 grams
Mary is starting the reaction with 216 grams. We need to convert this into moles in order to apply the mole ratio. One mole of ammonium carbonate has a formula weight of 96 grams. 216 grams / 96 grams per mole = 2.25 moles ammonium carbonate
We can now apply the mole ratio: 2.25 moles of ammonium carbonate will produce 4.5 moles of ammonia (NH_3).
We've been asked to find the number of grams produced. We need to convert our result from moles into grams. One mole of NH_3 has a formula weight of 17 grams.
*4.5 x 17 grams per mole = **76.5 grams NH_3.***

Name_____ Date_____

Friendly Chemistry

Lesson 29: Measuring Molar Volumes of Gases

1. You have learned that one mole of any gas at STP, occupies a volume of 22.4 liters. If Gina has 44.8 liters of a gas, how many moles of that gas does she have?

   One mole occupies 22.4 liters. 44.8 liters/22.4 liters = **2 moles of gas**.

2. Georgette collected 18 liters of neon gas. Does she have less than a mole, exactly a mole or more than a mole of neon?

   One mole of a gas has a volume of 22.4 liters.
   Georgette has less than one mole of neon gas.

3. Carbon dioxide gas is a product from the reaction of acetic acid (vinegar) and baking soda. Suppose you completed this reaction and found that you collected 50 liters of carbon dioxide at STP. How many grams of carbon dioxide did you produce in this reaction?

   First, we'll need to determine how many moles of CO_2 was produced. One mole of a gas at STP has a volume of 22.4 liters. We can set up this relationship:

   $$\frac{1 \text{ mole}}{22.4 \text{ L}} = \frac{X \text{ moles}}{50 \text{ L}}$$

   X = 2.23 moles. One mole of CO_2 has a mass of 44 grams. 2.23 x 44 grams = **98 grams of CO_2**. *(Note, if you round the number of moles you produced to 2.2 moles, your answer will be less than our 98 grams.)*

4. Tony had 12 moles of nitrogen gas (N_2). How many grams is this equal to?

   One mole of N_2 gas has a formula weight of 28 grams. 12 moles would, therefore, have a mass of ***336 grams***.

5. Argon gas is used between the glass panes of insulating windows. If the space between two panes of glass was equal to 3.5 liters, how many moles of argon gas could you inject at STP?

   One mole has a volume of 22.4 liters. We can set up this relationship:

   $$\frac{1 \text{ mole}}{22.4 \text{ L}} = \frac{X \text{ moles}}{3.5 \text{ L}}$$

   X = 0.16 moles

Friendly Chemistry

6. Potassium chloride and fluorine gas react to produce potassium fluoride and chlorine gas. If Patty begins with 24 moles of potassium chloride, how many liters of chlorine gas might she expect to produce in this reaction?

Here is our reaction: $2KCl + F_2 \longrightarrow 2KF + Cl_2$: Mole ratio is 2:1
Patty is beginning with 24 moles of KCl. By applying the mole ratio, we can predict that she will produce 12 moles of chlorine gas. We know that one mole of any gas at STP, has a volume of 22.4 L. Her 12 moles will, therefore, be equal to 12 moles x 22.4 liters per mole = **268 liters.**

7. When a person mixes calcium with water, calcium hydroxide and hydrogen gas are produced. If you begin with 400 grams of calcium, how many liters of hydrogen gas can you expect to produce from this reaction?

$\underline{Ca} + 2H(OH) \longrightarrow Ca(OH)_2 + \underline{H_2}$; 1:1 ratio
400 grams of Ca = 400/40 grams per mole = 10 moles of Ca. Applying the mole ratio we find that we will produce 10 moles of hydrogen gas. Each mole of hydrogen gas produced will have a volume of 22.4 liters. So, 10 moles x 22.4 liters per mole tells us this person will produce **224 liters of hydrogen gas.**

8. Tony had 90 milliliters of water. If he applied electricity to this water it would decompose to produce hydrogen gas and oxygen gas. How many liters of oxygen gas might he expect to produce from this 90 mls of water. He knew that one ml of water had the mass of 1 gram.
Here is our reaction: $\underline{2H_2O} \longrightarrow 2H_2 + \underline{O_2}$; 2:1 ratio
Tony's 90 mls of water = 90 grams of water. One mole of water has a weight of 18 grams. 90/18 grams per mole = 5 moles. Applying the mole ratio, we find that from our 5 moles of water, we will produce 2.5 moles of oxygen gas. Each mole of oxygen gas has a volume of 22.3 liters.
Therefore, 2.5 moles x 22.4 liters per mole = **56 liters.**

9. Potassium chlorate will decompose to produce potassium chloride and oxygen gas. If Hank began with 45 kilograms of potassium chlorate, how many liters of oxygen gas measured at STP might he expect to produce from his reaction?
Here is our reaction: $\underline{2K(ClO_3)} \longrightarrow 2KCl + \underline{3O_2}$; 2:3 ration or 1:1.5 ratio.
45 kilograms potassium chlorate = 45,000 grams potassium chlorate. One mole of potassium chlorate has a weight of 122 grams. 45,000 g / 122 grams per mole = 368 moles. By applying the mole ratio, we find that our 45,000 g of potassium chlorate will produce 552 moles of oxygen gas. Each mole has a volume of 22.4 liters. 552 x 22.4 liters per mole = **12,364 +/- grams**

10. How many atoms might you expect to find in 134.4 liters of helium gas?
134.4 liters of helium gas is equal to 6 moles (134.4 liters / 22.4 liters per mole). One mole = 6.02×10^{23} atoms. $6 \times 6.02 \times 10^{23}$ = **36.12×10^{23} atoms.**

NAME_____ DATE_____
FRIENDLY CHEMISTRY

Lesson 29 Test
Calculating Molar Volumes of Gases

Read each problem below carefully. Take your time and ask if you have questions.

1. Megan collected 44.8 liters of hydrogen gas at STP. How many moles of hydrogen gas did she have? Show your work for full credit.

   One mole of any gas at STP has a volume of 22.4 liters.
   *44.8 liters / 22.4 liters = **2 moles of hydrogen gas**.*

2. Travis added some magnesium pellets to a container of hydrochloric acid. He was able to capture 10 liters of hydrogen gas from the reaction. How many moles of hydrogen gas did he collect?

   One mole of any gas at STP has a volume of 22.4 liters.
   *10 liters / 22.4 liters = **0.45 moles of hydrogen gas.***

3. Ammonium nitrite decomposes to yield water and nitrogen gas (N_2). If you begin with 14 moles of ammonium nitrite, how many <u>liters</u> of nitrogen gas can you produce from this reaction?

   $(NH_4)(NO_2) \rightarrow 2H_2O + N_2$; Mole ratio is 1:1.
   We are beginning with 14 moles of ammonium nitrite and can go ahead
   And apply the mole ratio: 14 moles of ammonium nitrite will yield 14 moles of nitrogen gas. Each mole produced has a volume of 22.4 liters.
   *14 x 22.4 liters = **313.6 liters**.*

4. Trey mixed some charcoal (carbon) with some aluminum oxide. The reaction produced carbon dioxide gas and aluminum. If Trey used 60 grams of carbon, how many liters of carbon dioxide gas did he produce in his reaction?

Our reaction is: $\underline{3C}$ + $2Al_2O_3$ —> $\underline{3CO_2}$ + $4Al$; mole ratio is 1:1.
Trey began with 60 grams of carbon. We'll need to convert this into moles before applying the mole ratio. One mole of carbon has a weight of 12 grams. 60 grams / 12 grams per mole = 5 moles. Applying the mole ratio, we can say that 5 moles of carbon will produce 5 moles of carbon dioxide gas. Each mole of carbon dioxide gas produced has a volume of 22.4 liters at STP.
5 moles x 22.4 liters per mole = 112 liters.

5. Which is greater: 246.4 liters of oxygen gas or 176 grams of oxygen gas? Show your work for full credit.

We need to convert one of these amounts to the other. We chose to convert the 176 grams of oxygen gas to liters of oxygen gas. We know one mole of oxygen gas is equal to 32 grams. 176 grams / 32 grams per mole = 5.5 moles of oxygen gas. Each mole has a volume of 22.4 liters. 5.5 moles x 22.4 liters per mole = 123.2 liters.
Based upon these results, the 246.4 liters is the greater amount.

Name_____Date_____

Friendly Chemistry

Lesson 30: Charles's Law Practice –1
How Temperature Affects the Volume of a Gas

1. Tory had 5 L of helium gas at STP. If she heated the helium to 30 degrees C, what would the new volume of gas be?
    First, let's convert our temperatures to Kelvin: T_1= 0 degrees C + 273 = 273 K;
    T_2 =30 degrees C + 273 = 303 K
    The temperature rose, so we predict the new volume will be greater than 5L

    $$\frac{T_1}{T_2} = \frac{V_1}{V_2}$$
    $$\frac{273}{303} = \frac{5L}{X L}$$

    X = 5.5 L; our prediction was correct!

2. Amelia had 4.5 L of oxygen gas which was being held at 10 degrees C. If the gas was heated by 20 degrees C, what would the new volume of gas be?
    First, let's convert our temperatures to Kelvin: T_1= 10 degrees C + 273 = 283 K;
    T_2 =30 degrees C + 273 = 303 K
    The temperature rose, so we predict the new volume will be greater than 4.5L

    $$\frac{T_1}{T_2} = \frac{V_1}{V_2}$$
    $$\frac{283}{303} = \frac{4.5 L}{X L}$$

    X = 4.8 L; our prediction was correct.

3. Tim and Margaret each had a gas-filled balloon. The volumes of their balloons were exactly 2 L at STP. If Tim heated his balloon by 30 degrees K, what would the new volume of his balloon become?
    First, let's convert our temperatures to Kelvin: T_1= 273 K;
    T_2 =303 K
    The temperature rose, so we predict the new volume will be greater than 2L

    $$\frac{T_1}{T_2} = \frac{V_1}{V_2}$$
    $$\frac{273}{303} = \frac{2L}{X L}$$

    X = 2.2 L

4. Jack filled a balloon with 4 liters of carbon dioxide gas. The gas was at room temperature (25 degrees C). If he took it outdoors where the temperature was 4 degrees C, what would the new volume of the balloon be? Assume the pressure outside the house was the same inside the house.
    T_1= 25 degrees C + 273 = 298 K;
    T_2 =4 degrees C + 273 = 277 K
    The temperature fell, so we predict the new volume will be less than 4L

    $$\frac{298}{277} = \frac{4L}{X L}$$

    X= 3.7 L

5. Sheila worked in a lab which collected neon gas. Suppose she collected 45 liters of neon at 35 degrees C. If she cooled this gas to STP, what would be the new volume of the gas?

$T_1 = $ 35 degrees C + 273 = 308 K;
$T_2 = $ 0 degrees C + 273 = 273 K

The temperature fell, so we predict the new volume will be less than 45L

$$\frac{308}{273} = \frac{45L}{XL}$$

X = 39.9 L

6. Freddy purchased 14 L of argon gas at 28 degrees C. If he expected to store the gas at STP, how many L would he expect to need room for?

$T_1 = $ 28 degrees C + 301 = K;
$T_2 = $ 0 degrees C + 273 = 273 K

The temperature fell, so we predict the new volume will be less than 14L

$$\frac{301}{273} = \frac{14L}{XL}$$

X = 12.7 L

7. Mary Jo had a balloon filled with 0.5 liters of helium. If the temperature of the gas rose by 15 degrees, what would the new volume of her gas-filled balloon become?

$T_1 = $ 0 degrees C + 273 = 273 K;
$T_2 = $ 15 degrees C + 273 = 288 K

(Note that in the problem it did not give an actual starting temperature; we arbitrarily chose zero. However, we could have chosen just about any starting temperature as long as we added fifteen degrees to that value to get T_2.)

The temperature rose, so we predict the new volume will be greater than 0.5L

$$\frac{273}{288} = \frac{0.5L}{XL}$$

X = 0.53 L

8. Morris collected some hydrogen gas from an experiment he had conducted. He collected 12 L at a temperature of 28 degrees C. How many liters would this be equal to at STP?

$T_1 = $ 28 degrees C + 273 = 301 K;
$T_2 = $ 0 degrees C + 273 = 273 K

The temperature fell, so we predict the new volume will be less than 12 L

$$\frac{301}{273} = \frac{12L}{XL}$$

X = 10.8 L

Name_____ Date_____
Friendly Chemistry

Lesson 30: Charles's Law Practice –2
How Temperature Affects the Volume of a Gas

1. Calcium fluoride and sulfuric acid react to produce calcium sulfate and hydrogen fluoride gas. If you begin with 13 moles of calcium fluoride, how many liters of hydrogen fluoride gas measured at STP should you produce from the reaction?

   Our reaction is: $\underline{CaF_2}$ + $H_2(SO_4)$ —> $Ca(SO_4)$ + $\underline{2HF}$; Ratio is 1:2

   Since we are beginning with moles, we can go straight to applying the mole ratio. 13 moles of CaF_2 should produce 26 moles of HF gas.

   Each mole has volume of 22.4 liters, therefore 26 moles would have a volume of

   582.4 liters.

2. If the HF gas you produced in question 1 was heated <u>by</u> 40 degrees C, what would the new volume of HF be?

   T_1= 0 degrees C + 273 = 273 K

   T_2= 40 degrees C + 273 = 313 K

   $$\frac{273\ K}{313 K} = \frac{582.4\ L}{X\ L}$$

   X= 667.7 L

3. When strontium is placed into nitric acid (hydrogen nitrate), strontium nitrate and hydrogen gas are produced. If you begin with 58 grams of strontium, how many liters of hydrogen gas can you produce at STP?

   Our reaction is: $\underline{Sr}$ + $2H(NO_3)$ —> $Sr(NO_3)_2$ + $\underline{H_2}$; 1:1 ratio

   We are beginning with 58 grams of Sr which is equivalent to 0.66 moles Sr.

   Let's apply the mole ratio: 0.66 moles of Sr will produce 0.66 moles of hydrogen gas.

   One mole of any gas at STP has a volume of 22.4 liters, therefore 0.66 moles x 22.4 liters per mole = **15 liters of hydrogen gas**.

4. If the H_2 gas you produce in question 3 is heated <u>to</u> 25 degrees C, what will the new volume of gas become?

   T_1= 0 degrees C + 273 = 273 K

   T_2= 25 degrees C + 273 = 298 K

   $$\frac{273\ K}{298 K} = \frac{15\ L}{X\ L}$$

   X= 16.37 L

5. Iron (II) sulfide and hydrochloric acid react to produce iron (II) chloride and hydrogen sulfide gas. Suppose you begin with 1.5 kilograms of iron (II) sulfide, how many liters of hydrogen sulfide gas could you produce from this reaction assuming you conduct the reaction at STP?

$$\underline{FeS} + 2HCl \longrightarrow FeCl_2 + \underline{H_2S}; \text{ mole ratio is } 1:1$$

1.5 kg = 1500 g FeS. One mole of FeS = 88g. 1500g/88 grams per mole = 17 moles.

Applying the mole ratio: 17 moles of FeS yields 17 moles H_2S.

Each mole of H_2S produced has a volume 22.4 liters. Therefore, 17 moles x 22.4 liters per mole = **380.8 liters H_2S gas.**

6. Suppose you have 48 liters of this hydrogen sulfide gas at room temperature (25 degrees C.) If you cool this gas to STP, what would the new volume be?

$$T_1 = 25 \text{ degrees } C + 273 = 298 \text{ K}$$
$$T_2 = 0 \text{ degrees } C + 273 = 273 \text{ K}$$

Our temperature falls, so we would expect a decrease in volume.

$$\frac{298 \text{ K}}{273 \text{ K}} = \frac{48 \text{ L}}{X \text{ L}}$$

X = 43.9 L

NAME_____ DATE_____

FRIENDLY CHEMISTRY

Lesson 30 Test
How Changes in Temperature Affect the Volume of a Gas

1. Suppose you had 40 liters of methane gas at STP. If the temperature increased by 35 degrees C, what would the new volume of gas become?

$$\frac{T_1}{T_2} = \frac{V_1}{V_2}$$
$$\frac{273}{308} = \frac{40L}{X\,L}$$
X = 45.13 L

2. Sherry had 13.5 liters of oxygen gas measured at 25 degrees Celsius. She took the container that was holding the gas outdoors where the temperature was 10 degrees Celsius. What would the volume of gas become after it cooled?

$$\frac{T_1}{T_2} = \frac{V_1}{V_2}$$
$$\frac{298}{283} = \frac{13.5L}{X\,L}$$
X = 12.82 L

3. Francisco had a 46 liters of hydrogen gas at 37 degrees Celsius. If he changed the environment of the room to reflect STP conditions, what would the new volume of the hydrogen be?

$$\frac{T_1}{T_2} = \frac{V_1}{V_2}$$
$$\frac{310}{273} = \frac{46L}{X\,L}$$
X = 40.51 L

4. Hydrogen carbonate will decompose to produce water and carbon dioxide. Suppose you began with 45 grams of hydrogen carbonate, how many liters of carbon dioxide could you produce from this reaction assuming the reaction took place at STP?

Here is our reaction: $\underline{H_2(CO_3)} \longrightarrow H_2O + \underline{CO_2}$; Mole ratio is 1:1.
We are beginning with 45 grams of $H_2(CO_3)$. One mole of $H_2(CO_3)$ has a formula weight of 62 grams. 45 / 62 grams per mole = 0.73 moles. We can now apply the mole ratio: 0.73 moles of $H_2(CO_3)$ will yield 0.73 moles of carbon dioxide gas. Each mole of CO_2 gas has a volume of 22.4 liters.
*0.73 moles x 22.4 liters per mole = **16.35 liters CO_2 gas.***

5. If the carbon dioxide produced in question 4 was heated to 30 degrees C, what would the new volume of CO_2 be?

$$\frac{T_1}{T_2} = \frac{V_1}{V_2}$$
$$\frac{273}{303} = \frac{16.35 L}{X L}$$
X = 18.15 L

6. Carbon monoxide gas (CO) and oxygen gas will combine to produce carbon dioxide gas (CO_2). If you begin with 5 liters of carbon monoxide, how many liters of carbon dioxide can you produce from this reaction? Assume you conduct this reaction at STP.

Here is our reaction: $2CO + O_2 \longrightarrow 2CO_2$; mole ratio is 1:1.
We are beginning with 5 liters of CO. 5 liters / 22.4 liters per mole =
0.22 moles of CO.
We can now apply the mole ratio: 0.22 moles of CO will yield 0.22 moles of CO_2.
Each mole has a volume of 22.4 liters.
0.22 moles x 22.4 liters per mole = **5 liters of CO_2 gas.**

7. If the carbon dioxide gas you produced from the reaction in question 6 was heated to 200 degrees C, what would the new volume of gas be?

$$\frac{T_1}{T_2} = \frac{V_1}{V_2}$$
$$\frac{273}{473} = \frac{5 L}{X L}$$
X = 8.67 L

8. Shorty had 1 liter of 3 M hydrogen sulfate. If he added aluminum to this solution until the reaction stopped, how many liters of hydrogen gas could he produce from the reaction? Aluminum sulfate is a byproduct of the reaction. Assume the reaction took place at STP.

Here is our reaction: $3H_2(SO_4) + 2Al \longrightarrow 3H_2 + Al_2(SO_4)_3$; Mole ratio is 1:1.
Shorty's one liter of hydrogen sulfate will provide 3 moles for the reaction.
The mole ratio is 1:1, so 3 moles of hydrogen sulfate should yield 3 moles of hydrogen gas. Each mole of hydrogen gas has a volume of 22.4 liters.
Shorty should produce 3 moles x 22.4 liters per mole = **67.2 liters H_2.**

Name_____ Date_____

Friendly Chemistry

Lesson 31: Boyle's Law Practice
How Pressure Affects the Volume of a Gas

1. Terry has 17 liters of helium gas at 760 mm Hg. If he increases the pressure to 790 mm of Hg, what will the new volume of helium be? Assume there is no temperature change.

$P_1 = 760$ mm $P_2 = 790$ mm $V_1 = 17$ L $V_2 = X$ L

Pressure went up, we'd expect the volume to fall.

$$\frac{P_1}{P_2} = \frac{V_2}{V_1}$$

$$\frac{760 \text{ mm}}{790 \text{ mm}} = \frac{X}{17 \text{ L}}$$

X = 16.4 L

2. The current atmospheric conditions were 765 mm Hg. Marty had 5 liters of hydrogen gas. If the pressure changed to 740 mm of Hg, what would the new volume of hydrogen be? Assume there is no temperature change.

$P_1 = 765$ mm $P_2 = 740$ mm $V_1 = 5$ L $V_2 = X$ L

Pressure went down, we'd expect the volume to increase.

$$\frac{P_1}{P_2} = \frac{V_2}{V_1}$$

$$\frac{765 \text{ mm}}{740 \text{ mm}} = \frac{X}{5 \text{ L}}$$

X = 5.16 L

3. Darcy had a weather balloon with 10 liters of helium inside it. If she took it into the mountains where the pressure was 20 mm of Hg less than where she started, what will the new volume of helium be in her balloon. Assume there was no temperature change. $P_1 = 760$ mm $P_2 = 740$ mm $V_1 = 10$ L $V_2 = X$ L

Pressure went down, we'd expect the volume to increase.

$$\frac{P_1}{P_2} = \frac{V_2}{V_1}$$

$$\frac{760 \text{ mm}}{740 \text{ mm}} = \frac{X}{10 \text{ L}}$$

X = 10.27 L

Note: In this problem, we were not given a starting pressure, only that the starting pressure decreased by 20 mm. In this case, we just assigned a starting pressure (we chose 760 in this case) and then decreased that amount by 20 mm for P_2.

4. Josh had 34 liters of argon gas under a pressure of 770 mm of Hg. If the pressure changed to 790 mm of Hg, what would the new volume of argon be? Assume the temperature did not change.

$P_1 = 770$ mm $P_2 = 790$ mm $V_1 = 34$ L $V_2 = X$ L

Pressure went up; we'd expect the volume to decrease.

$$\frac{P_1}{P_2} = \frac{V_2}{V_1}$$

$$\frac{770 \text{ mm}}{790 \text{ mm}} = \frac{X}{34 \text{ L}}$$

$X = 33.1$ L

5. Sarah collected 500 ml of hydrogen from the reaction of zinc and hydrochloric acid. If she collected this at 1 atm of pressure but then pressurized the sample to 700 mm of Hg, how much space would the sample now require? Assume the temperature did not change.

$P_1 = 1$ atm $= 760$ mm $P_2 = 700$ mm $V_1 = 0.5$ L $V_2 = X$ L

Pressure went down, we'd expect the volume to increase.

$$\frac{P_1}{P_2} = \frac{V_2}{V_1}$$

$$\frac{760 \text{ mm}}{700 \text{ mm}} = \frac{X}{0.5 \text{ L}}$$

$X = 0.54$ L

Friendly Chemistry

NAME_____ DATE_____
FRIENDLY CHEMISTRY

Lesson 31 Test
How Changes in Pressure Affect the Volume of a Gas

1. Billy had 32 liters of hydrogen gas in tanks which measured 770 mm Hg. If Billy increased the pressure inside the tanks to 800 mm Hg, what would the new volume of hydrogen be inside the tanks? Assume no temperature change.

$P_1 = 770$ mm $P_2 = 800$ mm $V_1 = 32$ L $V_2 = X$ L

Pressure went up; we'd expect the volume to decrease.

$$\frac{P_1}{P_2} = \frac{V_2}{V_1}$$

$$\frac{770 \text{ mm}}{800 \text{ mm}} = \frac{X}{32 \text{ L}}$$

X = 30.8 L

2. Shelly put 5 liters of helium inside a weather balloon when the atmospheric pressure measured 765 mm Hg. The next day, the atmospheric pressure measured 760 mm of Hg. What would the new volume of helium be with this change in conditions?

$P_1 = 765$ mm $P_2 = 760$ mm $V_1 = 5$ L $V_2 = X$ L

Pressure went down; we'd expect the volume to increase.

$$\frac{P_1}{P_2} = \frac{V_2}{V_1}$$

$$\frac{765 \text{ mm}}{760 \text{ mm}} = \frac{X}{5 \text{ L}}$$

X = 5.03 L

3. Hank had 3 L of ammonia gas at 2 atm of pressure. If the pressure changed to 1520 mm of Hg, what would the new volume of ammonia be?

$P_1 = 2$ atm $= 1520$ mm $P_2 = 1520$ mm $V_1 = 3$ L $V_2 = X$ L

Pressure stayed the same! **Therefore, we'd expect no change in volume!**

$V_2 = 3.$ **L**

Name_____ Date_____
Friendly Chemistry

Lesson 32: Combining the Gas Laws

1. Suppose you collected 10 L of hydrogen gas from a lab experiment when the room temperature was 34 C and the atmospheric pressure read 762 torr. What would the volume of this hydrogen be at STP?

$$V_2 = V_1(T_2/T_1)\,(P_1/P_2)$$
$$V_2 = 10L\,(273/307)\,(760/762)$$
$$V_2 = 10L\,(0.89)\,(0.99)$$
$$\mathbf{V_2 = 8.8\ L}$$

2. Georgia had 3.5 L of argon gas at 33 C and a pressure of 733 torr. If she heated the gas to 40 C and decreased the pressure by 30 torr, what would the new volume of gas be?

$$V_2 = V_1(T_2/T_1)\,(P_1/P_2)$$
$$V_2 = 3.5L\,(313/306)\,(733/703)$$
$$V_2 = 3.5L\,(1.02)\,(1.04)$$
$$\mathbf{V_2 = 3.7\ L}$$

3. Sebastian combined zinc metal and hydrochloric acid to produce zinc chloride and hydrogen gas. If he collected 7 liters of hydrogen from this reaction when the room temperature was 24 C and the pressure was 755 torr, what would the volume be at STP?

$$V_2 = V_1(T_2/T_1)\,(P_1/P_2)$$
$$V_2 = 7L\,(273/297)\,(755/760)$$
$$V_2 = 7L\,(0.91)\,(0.99)$$
$$\mathbf{V_2 = 6.3\ L}$$

4. Tommy had 3.5 L of neon gas at 22 C. He heated it up to 32 C and increased the pressure to 780 torr. If the original pressure was 760 torr, what would the new volume of the neon be?

$$V_2 = V_1(T_2/T_1)\,(P_1/P_2)$$
$$V_2 = 3.5L\,(305/295)\,(760/780)$$
$$V_2 = 3.5L\,(1.03)\,(0.97)$$
$$\mathbf{V_2 = 3.49\ L}$$

5. Molly collected 10 liters of fluorine gas from a lab procedure. The room in which she collected it was at a temperature of 26 C. If she placed it into a cooler where the temperature was 20 C, what would the new volume of gas be. Pressures inside and outside the cooler were the same.

$$V_2 = V_1(T_2/T_1)\,(P_1/P_2)$$
$$V_2 = 10L\,(293/299)\,(760/760)$$
$$V_2 = 10L\,(0.88)\,(1)$$
$$\mathbf{V_2 = 9.8\ L}$$

6. How large would a 100 L sample of gas become if the pressure went from 760 torr down to 2 torr?

Our pressure falls drastically, therefore, we'd expect our volume to rise drastically.
$$V_2 = V_1\,(P_1 P_2)$$
$$V_2 = 100L\,(760/2)$$
$$\mathbf{V_2 = 38{,}000\ L}$$

NAME_____ DATE_____
FRIENDLY CHEMISTRY

Lesson 32 Test
Combining the Gas Laws

1. Margaret filled a balloon with 4.5 L of helium at a temperature of 35 C and at a pressure of 758 torr. The balloon had some instruments attached to it so it could send readings down to her when it was released. She let it go and at 300 feet up in the air, it sent her a message that said it was now 28 C and the air pressure was 740 torr. What would the new volume of the helium be?

$$V_2 = V_1(T_2/T_1)(P_1/P_2)$$
$$V_2 = 4.5\ L\ (301/308)(758/740)$$
$$V_2 = 10L\ (0.97)(1.02)$$
$$\mathbf{V_2 = 4.45\ L}$$

2. Hank collected 0.56 L of hydrogen gas from an experiment he had conducted. At the time of the collection the room temperature was 24 C and the atmospheric pressure was 752 torr. What would the volume of the hydrogen be at STP?

$$V_2 = V_1(T_2/T_1)(P_1/P_2)$$
$$V_2 = 0.56\ L\ (273/297)(752/760)$$
$$V_2 = 0.56L\ (0.91)(0.98)$$
$$\mathbf{V_2 = 0.49\ L}$$

3. Mary collected some oxygen gas from a reaction she did in the lab. She collected 35 L at a room temperature of 27 C and an air pressure of 745 torr. What would the volume of her oxygen be at STP?

$$V_2 = V_1(T_2/T_1)(P_1/P_2)$$
$$V_2 = 35\ L\ (273/300)(745/760)$$
$$V_2 = 35\ L\ (0.91)(0.98)$$
$$\mathbf{V_2 = 31.2\ L}$$

NAME_____DATE_____
FRIENDLY CHEMISTRY

Final Exam

A. Tell the following information about the element <u>calcium</u>:

1. Element symbol   **** = correct response

    A. C
    B. Ca ****
    C. Cl
    D. Co

2. Number of protons in one atom of this element

    A. 20 ****
    B. 40
    C. 60
    D. 80

3. Number of valence electrons

    A. 20
    B. 40
    C. 2 ****
    D. 10

4. Electronic configuration notation for calcium would have

    A. 20 arrows
    B. 10 arrows
    C. Subscripts which would add to 20
    D. Superscripts which would add to 20 ****

5. Electron dot notation for calcium would have

    A. One dot
    B. Two dots ****
    C. Four dots
    D. Twenty dots

6. The charge when calcium ionizes would be

    A. +1
    B. +2 ****
    C. -1
    D. -2

7. The calcium ion would be classified as a(n):

    A. Cation ****
    B. Anion

B. Using the ions barium and hypochlorite, answer the following questions.

8. The chemical symbol and charge for hypochlorite is

    A. $(ClO_1)^{+1}$
    B. $(ClO_1)^{-1}$ ****
    C. $(ClO_2)^{-1}$
    D. $(ClO_3)^{-1}$

9. The chemical formula for the compound barium hypochlorite would be:

    A. $Ba(ClO_1)$
    B. $Ba(ClO_1)_2$ ****
    C. $Ba(ClO_2)$
    D. $Ba_2(ClO_1)$

10. The number of grams found in one mole of barium hypochlorite is:

    A. 239 grams ****
    B. 223 grams
    C. 210 grams
    D. 251 grams

11. The percentage of barium hypochlorite made up by barium is:

    A. 13%
    B. 29%
    C. 57% ****
    D. 98%

Friendly Chemistry

C. For the next portion of this exam, refer to this reaction:

Potassium chloride and fluorine gas react to produce potassium fluoride and chlorine gas.

12. Choose the correctly balanced equation.

    A. KCl + F —> KF + Cl

    B. KCl + F$_2$ —> KF + Cl$_2$

    C. 2KCl + F$_2$ —> KF + Cl$_2$

    D. 2KCl + F$_2$ —> 2KF + Cl$_2$ ****

13. If you began with 4 moles of potassium chloride, how many moles of potassium fluoride might you end up with?

    A. 2 moles KF

    B. 1 mole KF

    C. 4 moles KF ****

    D. 8 moles KF

D. For the next portion of this exam, refer to this reaction:

Iron (III) nitrate and lithium hydroxide react to yield iron (III) hydroxide and lithium nitrate.

14. If you began with 360 grams of lithium hydroxide, how many grams of iron (III) hydroxide might you yield from this reaction?

    A. 535 grams ****
    B. 107 grams
    C. 24 grams
    D. 1070 grams

    Fe(NO$_3$)$_3$ + 3Li(OH) —> Fe(OH)$_3$ + 3Li(NO$_3$); 3:1 ratio. 360 g Li(OH) = 15 moles; apply mole ratio: 15 moles of LiOH will yield 5 moles Fe(OH)$_3$. One mole of Fe(OH)$_3$ has a mass of 107 grams. 5 moles x 107 grams per mole = 535 grams.

15. If you needed to prepare 1000 grams of iron (III) hydroxide from this reaction, how many grams of lithium hydroxide might you need?

    A. 673 grams ****
    B. 528 grams
    C. 107 grams
    D. 3000 grams

    Fe(NO$_3$)$_3$ + 3Li(OH) —> Fe(OH)$_3$ + 3Li(NO$_3$); 3:1 ratio. 1000 g Fe(OH)$_3$ = 9.3 moles Fe(OH)$_3$. Apply mole ratio: in order to prepare 9.3 moles of iron (III) hydroxide, we will need 28 moles of Li(OH). One mole of Li(OH) has a mass of 24 673 grams.

Friendly Chemistry

E. **For this part of the exam, refer to these solutions:**
   Solution A: 5 M solution of hydrogen chloride
   Solution B: 180 grams of hydrogen chloride dissolved in 1000 ml of water

16. Which solution has the greater molarity?

    A. Solution A
    B. Solution B
    C. They have the same molarity ****
    D. Solution C

    One mole of HCl = 36 grams.
    5 moles = 180 grams per liter
    They are the same!

17. If you had 500 milliliters of solution A, how many grams of hydrogen chloride would you have present in your sample?

    A. 2.5 grams
    B. 500 grams
    C. 90 grams ****
    D. 180 grams

    500 mls would have 1/2 the amount found in 1 liter (1000 mls). 180 / 2 = **90 g.**

F. **For the final portion of this exam, refer to the following information:**

   You have 5 liters of hydrogen gas at a temperature of 25 degrees Celsius and a pressure of 761 torr.

18. What would the volume of this gas be if the temperature increased to 30 degrees C?

    A. 16.2 liters
    B. 5.08 liters ****
    C. 10.4 liters
    D. 30 liters

    $\frac{T_1}{T_2} \quad \frac{V_1}{V_2}$
    $\frac{298}{303} \quad \frac{5L}{XL}$
    $X = 5.08 L$

19. If the pressure fell to 750 torr, would the new volume be greater, lesser or the same as the original 761 torr?

    A. Greater ****
    B. Lesser
    C. The same

    As the pressure falls, the volume increases.

20. What would the volume of this gas be at STP?

    A. 4.66 liters****
    B. 5.78 liters
    C. 5.21 liters
    D. 5.37 liters

    $V_2 = V_1(T_2/T_1)(P_1/P_2)$
    $V_2 = 5L (273/298)(761/750)$
    $V_2 = 5L (0.92)(1.01)$
    $V_2 = 4.66 L$

Useful Conversions

1 pound = 454 grams
2000 pounds = 1 ton
1 quart = 0.946 liters
2 pints = 1 quart
4 quarts = 1 gallon
2 cups = 1 pint = 16 fluid ounces
1 cup = 8 ounces
3 teaspoons = 1 Tablespoon
1 cubic centimeter (cc) liquid = 1 ml
1 inch = 2.54 cm
1 angstrom = 1×10^{-8} cm
1 micron = 1×10^{-6} meters

Temperature Conversions

Celsius to Fahrenheit: 9/5 (C) + 32
Fahrenheit to Celsius: 5/9 (F) - 32
Celsius to Kelvin: C + 273

Metric Prefixes

Mega = million
Kilo = thousand
Deca = ten
Deci = one-tenth
Centi = one-hundredth
Milli = one-thousandth
Micro = one-millionth

Made in the USA
Columbia, SC
11 July 2018